ENGLISH DEPARTMENT
St. Mary's College
na, -:- Minn ta

Modern Composition

Holt, Rinehart and Winston, Inc.
New York

BOOK 1

Modern Composition

by Wallace E. Stegner

Edwin H. Sauer

Jane Rummel

Contents

v

PART *II*   *Grammar and Usage*

Introduction

You may remember the first time you read something without anyone helping you. It was probably a story or a poem that an older person had read to you and that you had enjoyed enough to try reading by yourself. You may even remember what it was you read, although most people, if they remember the occasion at all, recall more clearly the joy of success in reading and less clearly the name of the story or poem.

On the other hand, few of you are likely to remember the first time you successfully wrote or composed something by yourself. In school you wrote stories and poems under the guidance of your teachers, and at home you wrote postcards or thank-you notes under the guidance of your parents. Perhaps you do remember some of these occasions. But your first attempt to write something by yourself is very probably an event you cannot recall.

There may be many reasons for your not remembering your earliest piece of writing. For one thing, the reason for this first attempt may have been relatively unimportant. Maybe it was a brief message to your mother about a telephone call or a list of some sort. It may have seemed too routine to be worth remembering.

In any case, since that time you have been constantly involved in the process of writing, both under the guidance of others and by yourself. Much of this effort may not seem like composition to you. You write short paragraphs in science and social studies, or even in music and art. Or you fill out forms on the first day of school, or make a grocery list, or write a note to a friend (including the forbidden in-class variety!). Still, these are all exercises in writing and all of them add a little to your skill.

Throughout life, whether we are in school or out, we are all concerned with ideas and the communication of these ideas. In our part of the globe and in much of the rest of the modern world, ideas are transmitted by reading and writing as well as by signs and spoken language. Even in those parts of the world where society is very primitive and there is little writing or reading, ideas exist and are communicated in some way.

The purpose of writing is to organize ideas for both the writer and the reader. The author of that first story that you read many years ago had an idea which he wished to convey. He organized his idea in such a way that you were able to understand it. The message that you left for your mother in your first scrawling attempt at written communication by yourself made sense to her because the idea was clear, even if the words were misspelled.

Writing or composition, then, is simply a way of organizing and expressing the thoughts you have. You have, of course, been practicing composition for some time. In this book, you will approach the craft of writing in a more direct, disciplined way. You will learn how to use familiar, everyday words and sentences to better express your ideas. The words are the same ones you have always used; the ideas—although growing in maturity and complexity—are the same ones you have been thinking about and talking over with others; it is the ways of fitting the words to the ideas that you will learn more about here.

PART *I*

Writing

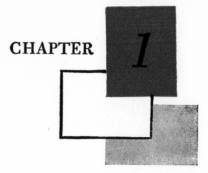

CHAPTER 1

The Importance of Writing

Here is a modern poem that you may enjoy.

> The Circus, or One View of It
> Said the circus man, Oh what do you like
> Best of all about my show—
> The circular rings, three rings in a row,
> With animals going around, around,
> Tamed to go running round, around,
> And around, round, around they go;
> Or perhaps you like the merry-go-round,
> Horses plunging sedately up,
> Horses sedately plunging down,
> Going around the merry-go-round;
> Or perhaps you like the clown with a hoop,
> Shouting, rolling the hoop around;
> Or the elephants walking around in a ring
> Each trunk looped to a tail's loop,
> Loosely ambling around the ring;
> How do you like this part of the show?
> Everything's busy and on the go;
> The peanut men cry out and sing,

The round fat clown rolls on the ground,
The trapeze ladies sway and swing
The circus horses plunge around
The circular rings, three rings in a row;
Here they come, and here they go.
And here you sit, said the circus man,
Around the circle to watch my show;
Which is show and which is you,
Now that we're here in the circus show,
Do you know? Do you know?
But hooray for the clowns and the merry-go-round,
The painted horses plunging round,
The live, proud horses stamping the ground,
And the clowns and the elephants swinging around;
Come to my show; hooray for the show,
Hooray for the circus all the way round!
Said the round exuberant circus man.
Hooray for the show! said the circus man.

(From *Poems*, 1940–1947 by Theodore Spencer, Harvard University Press, 1948. Copyright, 1941, by New Directions. Copyright, 1944, 1948, by The President and Fellows of Harvard College. Reprinted by permission.)

This is a lively, rhythmic poem, in which the writer has managed to include a great deal. The lines make us see the kinds of activities which go on inside the circus tent. We see the rings filled with horses going round and round, and with clowns and elephants and trapeze artists. The repetition of certain words ("around," "plunging," "rings," "row,") makes us feel the excitement of all the activity. Everywhere we look in the poem we can see a circle, and in every circle something is going on. "Everything's busy and on the go."

The writer has given us a vivid picture, but it is also a *moving* picture—a moving picture in words. Through the skillful use of words and of rhythm, the writer has been able to give us an experience very much like the real one of going to the circus. He has made his words and lines work on our imaginations, and we take genuine pleasure from what he has written as we recall our visits to the circus.

Surely the writer himself must have taken much pleasure from writing the poem. It is exciting to put words together, not only to express ideas but also to convey feelings. Writing is one of the most exciting things that men do. Great books, great speeches, and great letters have shaped history, and men have written these books, speeches, and letters in order that other men could read their ideas and, perhaps, act on them. But in the act of writing itself there is a great personal satisfaction. When we have finished a piece of writing, whatever it is, we know that we have *created* something—we have brought into existence something which did not exist previously. It is absolutely *ours*.

Much of the writing you do in school will be preparation for important writing which you will do later on—in high school courses, perhaps in college, and in your life after your school days are over. But try to think of your writing now as something more than just practical drill work. Think of it as something from which you can derive real enjoyment.

Though it has its very practical side, writing is also an art, and we can take pleasure from it just as we take pleasure from playing music or drawing a picture or taking a good photograph. Words are fascinating objects. They can be used in many patterns and arrangements. They can do wonderful and powerful things for you. Think of your work in composition as an opportunity to create something new and exciting. Think of writing as an activity intended, above all, to give pleasure to you and your reader.

Of course, there are other reasons for learning to write well, too. Writing is a skill that is needed by everyone. A person who writes well can express his ideas so clearly that everyone can understand him. In school, teachers will appreciate and students will benefit from a well-written paper.

Outside of school, people who read what you write—your friends, parents, and, in the future, your employers or employees—will appreciate being able to understand you. However, writing well, like playing tennis, or playing the piano well, requires practice. To be an expert, you have to keep at it. Try this exercise to practice your ability to communicate through writing.

Practice 1

You have probably all at one time or another performed various classroom duties, such as cleaning the chalkboard, straightening the desks, or leading the morning exercises. However, someone your age in, let us say, Iran or Paraguay has never had such duties. Perhaps he has never even seen a school.

Suppose now that you have to describe some such activity in writing to a foreign boy or girl. (You will have to assume, for the moment, that he or she understands English.) Write five or six sentences describing some class activity that is familiar to you but not to him. Perhaps you will want to put it in the form of a letter. Remember, he has probably never seen even a picture of a chalkboard!

Writing in school.   Throughout your school years, you will do more and more writing. Not only will you have more compositions and tests to write, but you will also find your personal writing increasing. One of your most important goals in the coming years should be to learn to write in such a way that other people actually look forward to reading what you have written.

Not long ago, some junior high school students were asked to list all the uses they have for writing, either at home or at school. They felt they should be able to express clearly in writing their knowledge and ideas in all classes and in the personal writing they might want to do. They then listed the following as the most important uses for writing:

1. Compositions and stories for English classes.
2. Reports for all classes: book reports, social studies reports, biographies of artists and scientists, and others.
3. Letters for home correspondence and letters for school "assignments."
4. Essay tests in all subjects.
5. Summaries and outlines, as well as analyses and interpretations of reading assignments.
6. Articles for the school newspaper.
7. Minutes of meetings and notes on oral presentations.
8. Exercises preparing for work in high school and beyond.

Here are some of the actual statements these students wrote in answer to the question, "Why learn to write?":

> I need writing in all my classes at school. In band I have to write a report on how a clarinet works. In algebra I use it for word problems. In English I need it for the type of paper I'm writing right now.
>
> At home I write stories and scripts for a drama group I attend. I enjoy writing letters and notes to friends.
>
> All in all, writing is a very important form of communication.
>
> Writing develops creativity and challenges the imagination.
>
> Some students find it difficult to put their thoughts on paper. By practicing in junior high, they get experience in organizing their ideas and in choosing words to express their thoughts clearly.

Writing, then, is a skill you use in many ways. First of all, you write often in your English class—compositions, book reviews, stories, short plays, and speeches. Second, you need to know how to write well in your other classes. Nearly every time you put your pencil to paper, you will be writing English, and you will need to know how to state your ideas clearly. You may know thoroughly the information required to answer a question, but you must also know how to present it in such away that your teacher will understand what you are trying to say. Teachers must be able to get your message.

At other times, you will be writing reports for your various classes. You should know how to organize the facts for these reports and how to write paragraphs that stay on the subject and really say what you want them to say. Your report will be better if you use proper manuscript form and if you summarize properly the reading you do in reference books. You will save yourself many headaches if you learn to use an outline as the "skeleton" for these reports, and even to write a rough draft. Perhaps most important, you should develop the habit of proofreading and of correcting, editing, and revising.

You will also be writing letters for different purposes. Perhaps you would like to write to a pen pal in Argentina, or to a friend who has moved away, or to a relative who always remembers your birthday. Maybe you have been visiting a friend or relative, or you have received a gift from someone. How do you write the thank-you note correctly?

You may want to write for the school newspaper. How do you write articles for the newspaper? Do you write a feature story and an editorial in exactly the same way? You may be elected to serve as secretary to a student organization. What facts should you include in the minutes of the meetings you are keeping?

From these examples of the kinds of writing that you will probably be doing in the next few years, you can understand the value and pleasure of writing. The seventh and eighth grades are good years to lay the groundwork for the four years of high school. Writing well will be even more important in the upper grades. The record you make in high school will be important to you whether you go on to college or right out to work. A knowledge of how to write will insure more success, whatever you do, after high school.

Those of you who may go on to college will have to take entrance examinations to qualify you for admission. In a recent article about the changing standards of 287 leading colleges, the College Board Association made this statement: "We are putting in this year what is called a writing sample—that is, an opportunity for a candidate for college to write for one hour— and the College Board will take this production and send it to the college or colleges to which the candidates apply. The college or colleges will undertake the judgment of it. So it's not an essay question in that sense of the word, but it is an opportunity to write."

Writing in modern society. Thus far we have discussed the more immediate reasons for improving writing ability. Such things as class work, extra-class work, personal letters, and reports or tests of any kind are all very important to help you gain success in your school years.

But the importance of learning to write well might be hard to see if these were the only reasons. As we have said, writing is a practical skill, a necessary one to have in day-to-day life, particularly in school life. However, writing is much more than just a skill. In many ways, it is preparation to be a useful and thinking member of society.

You have surely noticed that many topflight athletes, professional baseball, football, and basketball players, are often able to play many sports well. In your own school and in the high school to which you will go, there will probably be several students who are three-, four-, or five-letter men. The point is that athletes do not practice one game just for the sake of that game. They become skilled in all types of athletic activity and switching from one to another is very often just a matter of practice and experience. In short, an athlete trains his body not for one sport alone, but for an all-round vigorous life.

Writing is a skill which, in many ways, is similar. We do not learn to write just in order to do the immediate tasks, but rather to prepare ourselves for the life we hope to lead. In many ways, learning to write is learning to think. When we write, we put our thoughts on paper. If we were to put our ideas down just as they came to us, the result would too often be mere confusion. We have to organize our thinking. Learning how to write is basically a matter of learning how to organize our thoughts on paper, of learning *composition*.

Writing as communication. This textbook is called Modern Composition. Composition is a form of communication; it is putting the ideas we wish to communicate into intelligible form, so others may benefit from them. In some ways, it doesn't matter who it is we communicate with. We may even wish to communicate with ourselves. Many of the finest writers, as well as some of the greatest scientists and politicians and others, have made a practice of keeping a diary or journal. In the pages of these journals they communicate, as it were, with themselves, clarifying their ideas, and thus using writing as "a way of knowing." The important thing is being able to express our ideas.

Writing well, then, is a sign of the well-educated, thoughtful person. Such a person is the one who has ideas, who can put those ideas into some kind of order, and who is able to share them with others, and for whom the act of writing is a means of providing enjoyment and enrichment of his own life.

Practice 2

As a start in learning to write, you must have something to say. When you describe something, the reader must see it through your eyes. When you attempt to prove something, your own ideas must be convincing. Remember, too, that you hardly ever write just for exercise. Someone is going to read what you have said, and it is up to you to make it worth-while reading.

A. Read the following problem and then answer the question at the end.

In an election for class president, Hilda Petersen and Peter Corrallo are the two candidates. Hilda was vice-president last year. She is an excellent student and is a leading member of the drama club. She also lives in your neighborhood. You, however, know that she kept several girls out of the drama club last year because she felt "they didn't dress well enough."

Peter transferred to your school at the beginning of the year. He is an average student and does not work very hard. Everyone, both teachers and students, likes Peter, for he is a friendly and gentle boy. Furthermore, everyone admires his judgment and his natural ability for leadership. However, at the beginning of the year, Peter was suspended for a day because he was late to school every morning for three weeks.

In a short composition, perhaps one or two paragraphs, state your own preference in the election. Remember that you are also trying to convince others of the correctness of your choice.

B. Select one of the following ideas and write several sentences about it. Check these sentences over carefully when you finish and improve them in any way you think will make them more interesting for someone else to read.

  a) Introducing Me
  b) The Sport I Like Best
  c) My Favorite Book
  d) Getting Started at a New School
  e) The Kind of Gift I Like

C. Here are some sentences which you might use as the first sentence in a short piece of writing. They should provide you with some fun in trying to develop not only an idea but also a special feeling or mood.

  1. The water slowly inched toward my already sodden feet.
  2. The towering waves thundered against our shallow life raft.
  3. Bells, bells, bells—one more clang and I would go mad!
  4. The wall crumbled slowly until the deadly weight of its burden caused it to crash into the sea below.
  5. The only other person on the bus was an elderly man who kept talking aloud to himself.

D. Not all composition work is written. Speaking well is quite as important as writing well, and in a later chapter we deal in detail with effective speaking. For the present, see whether or not you are able to prepare, in not more than five minutes, a brief informal talk on a subject which is in the newspaper headlines right now. Prepare your talk in such a way that it will convince anyone who might hear you give the speech that your point of view is worth respecting.

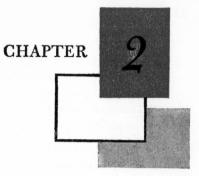

CHAPTER 2

The Kinds of Writing

Read carefully the following four paragraphs. How do they differ from one another?

1. All levels of education in Africa are dependent upon one another, as they are everywhere in the world. It is impossible to strengthen college education if the students sent on by the high schools are ill prepared. And it is obviously impossible ever to increase the size of the universities if the high schools do not produce enough graduates. A shortage of high schools is one of Africa's greatest educational problems, and at its heart is a serious lack of qualified teachers.

2. Bob ran to the door and opened it to find a stranger standing there, not his grandfather as he had expected. Before he could stop himself, he said, "Hi, Granddad." The stranger, who could not have been more than 25 years old, looked puzzled, then laughed. "Well, not quite yet, sonny," he said. "I'm the Fuller Brush man."

3. One of the most pleasing attractions in modern America is the fresh fruit and vegetable counter in a supermarket. At any time of the year a shopper can find nearly every fruit and vegetable which is grown anywhere on earth. Piles of

all kinds of apples are in one section, oranges, tangerines and lemons in another; berries, cherries and grapes abound, and there are melons even when you can see snow through the window. Rare and unusual vegetables are side by side with common ones. You can touch a potato with one hand and an artichoke with the other.

4. Driver education should begin in the junior high school even though students there are not old enough to qualify for a driver's license. The sooner a boy or girl learns the principles of safe driving and traffic regulation, the sooner he will be able to look out for himself in the modern world with its millions of cars on the streets and highways.

Each of these four paragraphs is actually different from the others in three important ways. For one thing, they tell about subjects or ideas that are different. Second, because of their differing main ideas, each paragraph has a differing *purpose*. That is, each paragraph is trying to do something different, such as just describe, explain, tell a story, or present an opinion. Third, the details in each paragraph are arranged in a different way, one that best carries out this purpose.

These four paragraphs illustrate the four main kinds of writing that you will be doing. Probably you noticed, for example, that in the first paragraph the writer gave you some important *information*. He explained something about African education. This kind of writing which explains is probably the most frequently used in modern life. It is called *exposition* or *expository writing*.

In the second paragraph you were told a little story or anecdote. The writer *narrated* an incident that took place. To narrate means to tell a story or give an account of an experience. This kind of writing is called *narration,* or *narrative writing.*

The third paragraph presents a picture of the fruit and vegetable counter in an American supermarket. It describes in detail what those counters look like and incidentally lends support to the opening statement that such counters are a pleasant and attractive sight. Such writing is called *description* or *descriptive writing.*

The last paragraph tries to convince the reader that driver education should begin sooner than it does. The writer is actually trying to *persuade* the reader to share his opinion.

Very often, a single piece of writing will be a combination of several kinds. It is easy and often necessary to combine narrative with description, or description with exposition, or exposition with persuasion. Good writing uses a variety of methods as you can see in the following selection.

One day when I was about ten years old and George eight, Father suddenly remembered an intention of his to have us taught music. There were numerous other things that he felt every boy ought to learn, such as swimming, blacking his own shoes, and bookkeeping, to say nothing of school work, in which he expected a boy to excel. He now recalled that music, too, should be included in our education. He held that all children should be taught to play on something, and sing.

He was right, perhaps. At any rate, there is a great deal to be said for his program. On the other hand, there are children and children. I had no ear for music.

Father was the last man to take this into consideration, however: he looked upon children as raw material that a father should mold. When I said I couldn't sing, he said nonsense. He went to the piano. He played a scale, cleared his throat, and sang *Do, re, mi,* and the rest. He did this with relish. He sang it again, high and low. He then turned to me and told me to sing it too, while he accompanied me.

I was bashful. I again told him earnestly that I couldn't sing. He laughed. "What do *you* know about what you can or can't do?" And he added in a firm, kindly voice, "Do whatever I tell you." He was always so sure of himself that I couldn't help having faith in him. For all I knew, he could detect the existence of organs in a boy of which that boy had no evidence. It was astonishing, certainly, but if he said I could sing, I could sing.

I planted myself respectfully before him. He played the

first note. He never wasted time in explanations; that was not his way; and I had only the dimmest understanding of what he wished me to do. But I struck out, haphazard, and chanted the extraordinary syllables loudly.

"No, no, no!" said Father, disgustedly.

We tried it again.

"No, no, no!" He struck the notes louder.

We tried it repeatedly.

I gradually saw that I was supposed to match the piano, in some way, with my voice. But how such a thing could be done I had no notion whatever. The kind of sound a piano made was different from the sound of a voice. And the various notes—I could hear that each one had its own sound, but that didn't help me out any: they were all total strangers. One end of the piano made deep noises, the other end shrill; I could make my voice deep, shrill, or medium; but that was the best I could do.

At the end of what seemed to me an hour, I still stood at attention while Father still tried energetically to force me to sing. It was an absolute deadlock. He wouldn't give in, and I couldn't. Two or three times I had felt for a moment I was getting the hang of it, but my voice wouldn't do what I wanted; I don't think it could. Anyhow, my momentary grasp of the problem soon faded. It felt so queer to be trying to do anything exact with my voice. And Father was so urgent about it, and the words so outlandish. *Do, re, mi, fa, sol, la, si, do!* What a nightmare! though by this time he had reduced his demands to my singing one single note: *Do.* I continually opened my mouth wide, as he had instructed me, and shouted the word *Do* at random, hoping it might be the pitch. He snorted and again struck the piano. I again shouted *Do.* (Reprinted from *The Best of Clarence Day*, by Clarence Day, by permission of Alfred A. Knopf, Inc. Copyright 1935 by Clarence Day, 1948, by Katherine B. Day.)

As you can see, the entire selection is a piece of narrative writing. The author tells us a little story, or part of a story, about his father's efforts to give singing lessons. Yet there are other kinds of writing used also. See if you can answer these questions.

1. Why did the author include the first paragraph; would the story have made as much sense if he had begun with the second paragraph instead? What kind of writing is the first paragraph?

2. What lines show that the author had to try to sing whether he wanted to or not? What lines in the fourth paragraph tell you that he was willing to try?

Why was he willing to try? What kind of writing would these lines be? Could they be any other kind of writing; if so, what kind?

3. What does the fifth paragraph tell you? What two kinds of writing are used here?

4. Look again at the following paragraph:

> I gradually saw that I was supposed to match the piano, in some way, with my voice. But how such a thing could be done, I had no notion whatever. The kind of sound a piano made was different from the sound of a voice. And the various notes— I could hear that each one had its own sound, but that didn't help me out any: they were all total strangers. One end of the piano made deep noises, the other end shrill; I could make my voice deep, shrill, or medium; but that was the best I could do.

These lines tell about the author's difficulty in understanding what he should do. What is the basic kind of writing used here? Are there any other kinds of writing used also? What are they?

As you can see, the four kinds of writing are often used to some extent in a single composition. But in order to know more about each of the four kindly let us look at them one at a time.

WRITING NARRATION

Narration, as you have seen, is an account of some incident or event; it is a story. Usually the aim of a narration is to give pleasure to the reader. The writer feels that what he is trying to say is interesting enough for others to know about.

In Chapter 7, you will learn more about the techniques of writing and telling stories. But, as you saw in the first sample paragraph on page 11, and as you can see in the following example, one of the most important things to remember in writing narrative is that the order in which things happen must be clear and correct. There must be no chance of the reader becoming confused about the way things have happened.

> The snake was swaying nearer; its tongue was darting in and out. Eben tried to summon his will power, tried to move farther back into the bush. Then, from somewhere floated a voice, the voice of a man speaking soft, low words. There were gentle footpads, and a hand touched the American on the shoulder. The voice continued; and now the cobra turned its swaying head and hood and proceeded with undulating motion toward the jungle grasses. (From "The Cobra's Hood" by Rupert Sargent Holland; Macrae-Smith Company.)

Notice the order of occurrence here: the snake sways nearer; the man tries to get away; a voice speaks; steps approach and a hand reaches out; the cobra turns and disappears. The incidents follow one another in a natural order. Since a story tells us about something that happened, the way that happening occurs is highly important.

Perhaps you noticed that an order of things happening means that there is a *time* sequence. If you relate what you do during a typical day, you will very likely use actual time of day to indicate when it is that you do particular things. Most of the time you would not say what you did in the evening, followed by what you had for breakfast, what you did in the afternoon, and then go back to what happened just before lunch. Unless you have some very special purpose in mind, such an arrangement of events could be very confusing.

A good way to be sure that the incidents you tell about are in the right order is to list them briefly in that order before you start writing. (You will read more about outlining in Chapter 6). Another advantage to putting your ideas down in this way is that you can see the beginning and the end of your story. Look again at the sample paragraph on page 16 and at the outline given immediately afterward. The incident opens with the snake swaying nearer, and it ends with the snake going away.

Finally, a narrative is interesting if it does more than merely tell what happened. How does the writer or the main character feel about what is happening? Eben, in the sample paragraph on page 16, was obviously very frightened, and the paragraph showed how frightened he was. The snake didn't just come closer; it swayed and its tongue darted in and out. Such details are, of course, descriptive details and they do much to increase the interest of a paragraph.

Practice 3

A. Complete the following story and give it a title.

> One beautiful spring day Peter and Wally decided to go on a nature walk. They enjoyed walking through the woods back of their home and they very often came home with interesting plants, bits of moss or lichen, or strangely shaped and colored stones.
>
> On this particular excursion, Peter walked ahead of Wally, stopping here and there to examine a stone or some interesting plant. He turned to make a remark to Wally, but Wally was nowhere in sight. Peter went back to find him, and, just as he came to the small clearing in the woods where they had stopped a few minutes before, he heard a whirring sound. He looked up and to his astonishment saw . . .

B. Write a paragraph that tells about an important or exciting play in a baseball, basketball or other game that you have recently seen. Perhaps you saw it on television or in person. Be sure you have the order of details correct and that you have a beginning and an ending. If possible, write it as if you were reporting the play as a sportswriter might, giving it as much color and interest as you can.

C. Write a narrative composition of one of the following topics:
   The Time I Fell Out of Bed (or some other experience)
   How I Earned My First Dollar
   How I Spent the First Dollar I Earned

WRITING DESCRIPTION

Sometimes you will want to describe a place, a person, or a thing in a completely factual way. This kind of description would be needed if you were ordering something by mail, especially if you had no catalog to refer to. You would have to have your facts just right in order to make your wishes perfectly clear.

When you do this kind of writing you must be accurate and exact. You are writing for a very practical reason and a poor description would be worthless. You must be sure that you have not overlooked any feature of the person, place or thing which might help someone to identify or recognize it. In short, you must make your description complete.

At other times your descriptive writing will be done to give pleasure as well as to identify. Perhaps you have seen a place, such as a room, a particular street, a lake or a countryside, which appealed to you so much that you would like a friend to enjoy it, too. Here you would try to recapture the appearance of the place by describing it for him.

Such description is called imaginative description and it tries to appeal to the senses. It uses colorful words and images so that your reader can use his imagination to see, or even taste, feel, hear or smell the place or object. Notice how the following description appeals to the eye with color and light.

> The palace of the Sun was a radiant place. It shone with gold and gleamed with ivory and sparkled with jewels. Everything without and within flashed and glowed and glittered. It was always high noon there. Shadowy twilight never dimmed the brightness. Darkness and night were unknown. Few among mortals could have long endured that unchanging brilliancy of light, but few had ever found their way thither. (From "Phaëthon," by Edith Hamilton; from

Mythology. Little, Brown & Co., copyright 1940 and 1942
by Edith Hamilton.)

Generally, when you do this kind of writing, you should try to see the place as a picture, much as the author of the above paragraph did. There should be some kind of focus, that is the object or place should be seen in relation to other objects or places. Here, the focus uses comparison with everything that is light and bright. The author has made the palace seem far brighter in comparison to anything else the reader may have experienced.

In the sample paragraph about fruits and vegetables given on page 11, the writer moves from one place to another. He focuses first on the apples in one section and then on the oranges, lemons and tangerines in another. He moves from common vegetables such as potatoes to less common, such as artichokes. Throughout he compares the usual to the unusual: all of these fruits and vegetables may be found even when they are out of season.

One writer said of description: "If you are describing a house as seen from a cliff a mile away from the house, you must describe it as it looks from that distance. You destroy the scale and make the description ridiculous if at the distance of a mile you give the color of the window curtains." Notice how the author of the description of the palace of the Sun abides by this statement. She is describing a mythological place, one that she nor anyone else has ever seen. Therefore, she gives only those details that can be imagined by each reader in his own way; there is no minute or exact description of the floor or the ceiling or the courtyard.

Good imaginative description starts with selection. We do not try to include all the details, but only those which create the effect we want, as a painter selects.

Remember that factual description is like a photograph, while imaginative description is like a painting.

Practice 4

A. Go to a window in your house and study the view from it. Then write a paper of about six sentences describing what you see. In this composition tell what direction the window faces and describe clearly and in some order the objects you see. You may want to go from left to right, or from near to far. Include any sounds, or smells you notice.

B. Using your senses of sight, touch, sound, or smell, describe in a few sentences a simple object, such as a brick, a pail of water, a shoe, or a patch of moss. Your description should be in very specific terms. Thus, if you say that the moss is green, tell *how* green it is.

C. Write one paragraph of description on one of these topics.

1. You are standing on the side watching a Fourth of July or other parade go by.
2. You are watching the "home crowd" leaving after the loss of the big game.
3. You are in a railroad station, a bus terminal, an airport or other public place on the day before a big holiday.

WRITING EXPOSITION

Exposition, or the kind of writing which explains, often tries to answer one or more of the following questions.

1. What is it? (a mail order catalog)
2. What is it meant to do or be used for? (a book of etiquette)
3. How well does it fulfill its intended function? (a report card)
4. When did it happen or when did it exist? (an accident report)
5. How did it come to be this way? (a note from home explaining absence)
6. How is it put together? (a cook book)
7. How does it work? (a manual for operating a lathe)
8. What does it mean? (an editorial)
9. What is its worth? (an advertisement)
10. What is its importance? (a museum guide book)

As you can see from the variety of things which answer the questions that exposition deals with, exposition is a common kind of writing. You encounter it every day, in school through textbooks of all kinds—this textbook that you are reading is largely exposition—and at home in a variety of ways, in recipes, labels, direct mail advertising, and in much of the material you may see in newspapers and magazines. Exposition serves a variety of needs: defining a word, telling how to get to a street address, giving the structure of a flower, explaining the working of a watch, interpreting the meaning of an historical event, excusing our behavior, or telling the meaning of an idea.

Exposition, like all other kinds of writing, is seldom used all by itself. To explain something, you often have to describe it. To persuade someone, you often have to explain what it is you are arguing about. When you do explain something, it is quite important that you be as clear as possible. There must be order to your explanation; a recipe given backwards could be disastrous!

More than in any other kind of writing, perhaps, exposition demands a plan of operation. In Chapter 6 on pages 78–82, you will find much more thorough material on how to make an outline. But there are some very basic steps you should follow in planning an expository composition.

First, decide which one or two of the ten questions your composition will seek to answer. Will you tell what it is, how it works, or how much it is worth? In most cases, the answer will be obvious, but still it is wise to remind yourself what it is you are going to be doing when you write. What you will have done is determine the *purpose* of your composition.

Then, list the details that are necessary to your explanation. The order of these details is, of course, important, and, as you make your list and later as you write your composition, you will see how each detail can lead naturally to the next. Thus, you need to fix not only the details but also the order in which the details will be used.

Finally, you need to select the important from the unimportant. In describing a horseshoe, for instance, it is hardly necessary to give much detail about a horse or the history of blacksmiths. Go through your outline as you work on your composition, and decide what materials are essential and which ones are not. In this way you will limit your topic properly and stress only the most important details.

Practice 5

A. How do you tie your shoe? Assume that you must write an explanation to be distributed to people who have never worn anything but sandals or a similar type of shoe or who have gone without shoes. Tell them exactly how to tie a shoelace.

B. If you ride a bicycle, you are aware that flat tires are a common problem. In a paper of five to six sentences, tell how to change a flat tire. Since the rear tire is a more complicated matter, describe only the process for changing the rear tire.

WRITING PERSUASION

Writing which presents an opinion usually follows a simple plan.

1. It states an opinion.
2. It presents facts, examples, and reasons to support the opinion.
3. It summarizes the opinion.

The example on page 12, arguing in favor of junior high school driver education follows this plan, as you will see if you look back.

Persuasion nearly always depends for its effect on clear exposition of the facts, examples and reasons that support the opinion. The facts must be accurate and reliable, and they must be convincing arguments. Notice how the author of the following selection uses reliable figures as well as impressive arguments to build up to the conclusion he wishes to make.

Today, with aid of modern inventions—the typewriter, the dictaphone, the Braille slate, the Talking Book, the radio—blind people are better equipped than ever before to take their place as competent members of society. The employable blind, 40,000 of them, ask for the confidence of the public. Without that confidence all the progress which has been made toward changing them from liabilities to potential social assets will have been in vain. They do not ask for pensions, for sentimental charity. They want only that opportunity to live a full life socially and economically which is the birthright of every American. (From *The World At My Fingertips* by Karsten J. Ohnstad, The Bobbs-Merrill Company, 1942. Copyright, 1942, by Karsten J. Ohnstad. Reprinted by permission of Karsten J. Ohnstad.)

Writing persuasion demands that you write fairly and clearly. To write fairly, you must be sure that what you say is accurate and that it provides *all* the necessary facts to allow your reader to judge for himself whether or not he agrees with you.

Practice 6

A. Decide whether or not you agree with this statement:

"School hours should be extended so that classes begin at 8:30 A.M. and end at 4:00 P.M. However, with the longer hours, all homework will be eliminated."

Now write a composition of five or six sentences giving arguments for or against this proposal. Remember that you are trying to persuade someone to accept your opinion.

B. In a composition of one or two paragraphs *defend* or *oppose* any one of the statements listed below. You need not count words since quality is more important than quantity. Be sure that your argument is logical:

1. Junior high school pupils should be allowed to have work permits.
2. Too much emphasis is placed on grammar in English courses.
3. Women's fashions (or hair styles) are getting stranger every year.

C. Nearly everyone has a hobby. Assume that the person sitting next to you does not particularly like your hobby. In a well-organized paper of six or seven sentences bring out the most convincing points you can think of to make him change his mind.

CHAPTER 3

Words and Their Meanings

A writer uses words as a mason uses bricks. They are his basic materials. He creates word pictures with them, just as a mason creates a building or a wall with his bricks. To create his building or wall, a mason needs bricks that have been molded firmly and evenly. To create his word pictures, a writer needs words that sparkle and sing, words that have freshness and zip.

Many of the words we use now we were never aware of learning. All of us began to talk and to use words by imitation, of our parents, older brothers and sisters, and friends. But, if we were to depend solely upon the words that we hear, our vocabularies would be sadly limited. In fact, we probably could not write down any but the simplest ideas. Therefore, in order to increase our word power, we have to learn other ways of adding to our supply.

Just reading will increase a vocabulary. Books, magazines, signs, all manner of printed materials have unfamiliar words which you often learn just by using them. But, there are ways and means which you can use to speed up the process a little, and to make sure that the words you have begun to learn become active parts of your vocabulary. This is important since the more words you know and can handle easily, the more power you have in your speech and writing.

THE DICTIONARY

A good dictionary is a student's best friend and, if properly used, will be of tremendous help to you as you add to your word supply. Just like getting started in a new school, getting acquainted with a dictionary requires some effort. But the time needed to get acquainted will be time well-spent.

Most dictionaries will contain the following basic information.

The meaning of words. In unabridged dictionaries, all the possible meanings of every word listed are given. In the smaller dictionaries, only the most important and useful meanings are listed. Parts of speech are indicated by abbreviations (*n.*, *v.*, *adj.*). If a word can function as more than one part of speech, the meanings and proper use of each are given.

The spelling and pronunciation of words. You can depend upon the dictionary to give you the proper spelling of any word you look up. In case a word has more than one acceptable spelling, the most common spelling is listed first. If a word has other functions, such as a noun, verb, adjective, or adverb, the changes in spelling are given. You will also find each word broken into syllables with the accented syllables marked (e.g., hick′o·ry). To help you pronounce the word, it will then be spelled as it sounds, with the vowels marked according to a pronunciation key that you can usually find on the inside of either the front or back cover (hĭk′ô·rĭ).

The history of words. Sometimes it is useful to know if a word has come from Latin, Greek, or some other language. Many dictionaries trace a word through several different stages and languages, so that its development in English is clear. This information about a word is called its "etymology."

The proper use of words. For many words included in a dictionary, a note is added to show that the word is not generally acceptable in standard written English. An example is the word "ain't," which is not considered good usage. Such words are often labeled "dialect," "nonstandard," "slang," or "colloquial."

Other information, such as the meanings of names, translations of foreign expressions, geographical and biographical terms, is given, depending upon the size and scope of the dictionary.

Quite obviously, the dictionary is too large a book for anyone to study from start to finish. As a matter of fact, it would do you little good to use it that way. Probably the best way to use a dictionary is to consult it often, and properly, whenever you have a need to do so.

Practice 7

A. Look up these words in your dictionary. Notice that, as the function and meaning of each word change, the pronunciation often changes as well. Write sentences that show at least two different functions of each word. Be prepared to read your sentences aloud, pronouncing the word correctly.

1. recall
2. appropriate
3. delegate
4. moderate
5. produce

B. Whenever you need to divide a word at the end of the line, you should divide it between syllables. (Refer to page 219, Chapter 13). Divide the following words into syllables. Then check your results against the dictionary.

1. government
2. ambulatory
3. discrimination
4. repeat
5. connect
6. explanation
7. electrode
8. rhinoceros
9. each
10. ambivalent

C. Can you pronounce the following words? Check in your dictionary to find the proper way. Learn the symbols used in the dictionary to describe the proper pronunciation of a word.

1. crochet
2. knave
3. whey
4. stomach
5. either
6. undoubtedly
7. obnoxious
8. psychiatry
9. bequeath
10. inquiry

D. For some words that can function as more than one part of speech, the spelling changes, but for others it does not. The only way to determine the function of the word is by the way it appears in the sentence. For each of the following words find how many different parts of speech are listed. Choose one of them and write two paragraphs of about five sentences each to show two meanings and uses of the word.

1. digest   4. tender
2. blank   5. quiet
3. court

E. Find the origin and history of the following words in your dictionary.

1. satellite   4. submarine
2. sovereign   5. debt
3. telescope

F. Now try the following questions. See how many answers you know already and then look up the others in the dictionary.
  1. Which of the following would excite a *numismatist:* old coins, rare stamps, a hot fudge sundae?
  2. What is the chief weapon of the peaceful *hedgehog?* Are all hedgehogs animals?
  3. If you found yourself in a *quandary*, would you look for a ladder, a counselor with good judgment, or somebody with a parachute?
  4. Which of the following is most likely to eat worms and flap its wings: the *jaywalker*, the *hawksbill*, or the *flycatcher?*
  5. A *phoebe* is a bird. Poets have also given this name to the moon. But how in the world does one pronounce it?
  6. The word *corps* is often mispronounced. According to the dictionary, should the word rhyme with "warps" or with "door"?
  7. Why do we use the word *stoic* when describing someone who hides pain or grief?
  8. What links the words *sandwich* and *cardigan* to English nobility?

9. How did the flowers *begonia* and *magnolia* get their names?

10. A *protozoan* is a one-celled animal. If you were trying to catch one, would you look in the sea, in a babbling brook, or in stagnant water?

HAVING FUN WITH WORDS

Have you ever seen a Meccano set? The set contains metal pieces of all shapes and sizes with holes punched in them; nuts and bolts enable you to hold the pieces together for making bridges or other structures. However, each piece in the box is useless and uninteresting by itself, and it is only when you put the pieces together that you have fun.

The words in your language are very much like the pieces in the Meccano box. You can create effects with them just as you can construct projects with Meccanos.

The poet Ogden Nash does this often. He has this to say about the Abominable Snowman:

> "I've never seen an abominable snowman,
> I'm hoping not to see one,
> I'm also hoping, if I do,
> That it will be a wee one."

> (Copyright 1956 by Ogden Nash; originally
> appeared in *The New Yorker*.)

In this verse about the wasp, note how he invented a word to fit his need:

> "The wasp and all his numerous family
> I look upon as a major calamity.
> He throws open his nest with prodigality,
> But I distrust his waspitality."

> (Copyright 1942
> by Ogden Nash)

Ogden Nash is famous for inventing new words for the sake of humor. Another common device that a humorist frequently uses is the pun. A pun results from using a single word with a double meaning to create a humorous effect. Here is an example:

> "Is life worth living?
> That depends on the liver."

Practice 8

A. Write a humorous four-line poem in the manner of Ogden Nash. Don't hesitate to invent a new word if you need to.

B. Bring to class puns that you see in newspapers or periodicals, or that you hear on radio or television. Can you explain their "humor"?

Words and rhythm

Even drill sergeants have used words humorously to train their soldiers. One sergeant wrote the following verse to help his soldiers keep in step:

> "The captain rides in a jeep,
> The colonel rides in a truck,
> The general rides in a limousine,
> But you're just out of luck.
> Sound Off! One Two
> Sound Off! Three Four
> Cadence Count
> One Two Three Four
> One-two - — - Three-four."

The singsong cadences of the "caller" at a barn dance have a similar rhythm.

> "Swing your partner.
> Do si do
> Swing her high,
> Swing her low.
> With an allemand left
> And an allemand right,
> Swing your partner
> Do si do."

The rhythm in the words is so catchy that no one can resist it. Here are two selections from well-known poems. Note how Alfred Noyes used words and rhythms to heighten the effect he was trying to create in "The Highwayman."

"The wind was a torrent of darkness among the gusty trees,
The moon was a ghostly galleon tossed upon cloudy seas,
The road was a ribbon of moonlight over the purple moor.
And the highwayman came riding—
    Riding-riding—
The highwayman came riding, up to the old inn-door."

(From *Collected Poems, Volume I,* by Alfred Noyes. Copyright 1906, 1934 by Alfred Noyes. Published by J. B. Lippincott Company.)

Edgar Allan Poe created a "tinkling" effect in "The Bells."

"Hear the sledges with the bells—
    Silver bells!
What a world of merriment their melody foretells!
How they tinkle, tinkle, tinkle,
    In the icy air of night!

*   *   *   *   *

Keeping time, time, time,
In a sort of Runic rhyme,
To the tintinabulation that so musically wells
    From the bells, bells, bells, bells,
        Bells, bells, bells—
From the jingling and the tinkling of the bells."

Practice 9

A. Try your hand at combining words and rhythm to create some effect in verse. The effect may be humorous, jolly, or even sad. However, a sad poem requires a slow, heavy rhythm rather than a quick, bouncy one.

B. Words are the magicians of the advertising business. A glance at a single copy of a newspaper or magazine, even at one program on television, can easily demonstrate the power of words in ads, and sometimes effect is more important than grammar!

"Luxuria" is a beauty cream with just a hint of snob appeal in its name. "Tanfastic" is the name of a suntan lotion. "Fasteeth" is the name of a powder to hold false teeth in place. "Lid-flippers" are bargains that will really excite the customer. "Young Promise" is the name of a cream that will "fight aging." "Expando" is the name of a trailer home. The name of the "Secured Mortgage Company" gives its customers a nice safe feeling. All such ads depend upon the power of words to influence customers in favor of their products. How many more examples can you find in your newspapers and magazines?

C. Here is a chance to use your word power.
   1. Invent some new words as brand names for items such as a baseball bat ("hitstraordinary"), soap ("gleamclean"), or any others that come to mind.
   2. Try your hand at writing some ads. Name the product, and "sell" it in three sentences or less.
   3. Write a commercial for an imaginary product, perhaps using a jingle.
   4. Use the form of one of the commercials on television to make up a commercial of your own.
   5. You are a salesman who is trying to interest a customer in a "Goofproof" can opener. Write a dialogue and give it for the class. For fun, play both parts, changing hats and pitch of voice to indicate change in speakers.

WORD ANATOMY

Just as the doctor must know the anatomy of the human body in order to understand better how it functions, so the writer must know the anatomy of words in order to understand better how they function. Just as glands and small organs affect the functions of the principal organs, so do *affixes* affect the functions of words. An affix is an addition to the main part of the word. A knowledge of these affixes and how they affect the meaning of the word is very important and useful for you.

The main part of the word is called the *root*. Roots come from many foreign languages, in greater part from Latin and Greek. One of the common roots is *port,* from the Latin word *portare,* meaning *to carry.* Some words that contain this root are: *transport, deport, portable, import, export, report,* and *support.* Notice that affixes have been added to the root, either before or after it. These additions change the meaning of the root. Notice the endings and how they alter the meaning of the root, *port;* in many cases the original meaning of "carry" has been changed.

Prefix	Root	Suffix	Meaning
trans	port		carry across
de	port		send [away] from
	port	able	can be carried
im	port		bring into
ex	port		send out of
re	port		tell back, give an account of
	port	er	one who carries

If the affix comes before the root, it is called a **prefix.** If it is added after the root, it is called a **suffix.** The suffix not only changes the meaning of a word, but it also changes the classification of the function of the word in a sentence. For example, the word "transport" shows action and thus is classified as a verb, but transport*ation* names the act itself and thus is classified as a noun. Port*able* has an ending, *able,* that indicates that this word tells something more about a noun and is therefore an adjective. Think of a "portable" typewriter or phonograph.

Here are other examples of root words and the affixes which change their functions in the sentence:

re*spect* = esteem or honor (noun); to esteem or honor (verb)
in*spect* = to look into (verb)
in*spec***tor** = one who looks into (noun)
*spec***tacle** = something to look at (noun)

Prefixes. The prefixes on the following page are used in forming English words. Consult the dictionary for more examples of the use of each prefix. Notice how they change the meanings of the root words.

Prefix	Meaning	Example	Meaning
a, ab	from, away, not	atypical	not typical
ante	before	anteroom	a room that comes before another room
anti	against	antitoxin	a serum that fights against disease
auto	self	automobile	moves by itself
bi	two	bicycle	a two-wheeler
co	with	co-operate	to work together
de	from	defrost	to free from frost
dis	not	discomfort	no comfort
e, ex	out of	exit	a place to go out
in	not	incomplete	not complete
inter	between	international	between nations
intra	within	intramural	within an institution or group
mis	wrong	misspent	spent wrongly or foolishly
post	after	postscript	written after the main part of something
pro	forward	produce	bring forward
re	back	retrace	trace back
semi	half	semicircle	a half circle
sub	under	submarine	under the sea
super	beyond	supernatural	beyond the natural
trans	across	transfer	to carry across
un	not	unable	not able

A group of prefixes that means "not" or "the opposite" is: *un, in, im, il, ir, dis,* and *mis.* You can change the meanings of words to the exact opposite by adding one of these prefixes. A word that means the exact opposite of another is called an antonym (see pages 40–41). For example, the antonym of "happy" is "*un*happy."

Suffixes. Suffixes are word endings which change the meaning of the stem or root of a word and change its part of speech. Here is a partial list of suffixes that usually indicate a noun:

Noun Suffix	Meaning	Example	Meaning
an	one who, native of	American	one who is a citizen of America
ance, ence	state of being	attendance independence	the state of attending the state of being independent
ary (see adj. list also)	that which, place for	library	a place for books
dom	power of, state of	freedom	the state of being free
ery	that which, place where	stationery	that which stationers sell
hood	state or rank	manhood	the state of being a man
ism	state or quality	patriotism	the quality of a patriot
ist	one who	dentist	one who cares for teeth
ment	resulting state or condition	resentment	the state of resenting
ness	quality or state of being	kindness	the quality of one who is kind
or, er	one who, that which	actor lawyer	one who acts one who practices
ship	state or quality of being	friendship	the state of being a friend
tion	state of, result of	civilization	the state of being civilized

The suffixes below and on the next page indicate that the word is very likely an *adjective:*

Adjective Suffix	Meaning	Example	Meaning
able, ible	capacity of being	lovable	capable of being loved
al	pertaining to, like	royal	like a king
ary, ory	pertaining to, like	introductory	pertaining to the introduction

Adjective

Suffix	Meaning	Example	Meaning
en	of the nature of	wooden	like wood
ic	pertaining to, like	comic	like a comedian
ical	pertaining to, like	historical	pertaining to history
il, ile	pertaining to, like	juvenile	like a youth
ish	of the nature of	foolish	like a fool
less	without	hopeless	without hope
ous, ious	full of	joyous	full of joy

The following suffixes often indicate that the word is a *verb:*

Verb

Suffix	Meaning	Example	Meaning
ate	to make or do	placate	to make happy
fy	to make	magnify	to make larger
ize	to make like	dramatize	to make like a play

The following suffixes may indicate that the word is an *adverb:*

Adverb

Suffix	Meaning	Example	Meaning
er	more (in degree)	shorter	more short
est	most (in degree)	latest	most late
ly	manner, like	friendly	as a friend
most	highest (in degree)	uppermost	most outstanding

Stems (Roots). The *stem* or *root* of the word is the basic element containing the central meaning. Many English words contain stems borrowed from Latin and Greek. A knowledge of both stems and affixes will give you a better understanding of the precise meaning of these words. A few useful stems are listed below and on the next page.

Stem	Meaning	Example	Meaning
meter	measure	thermometer	heat measure
ped	foot	pedal	concerning the foot

Stem	Meaning	Example	Meaning
fort	strong	fortress	a strong place
cred	to believe	incredible	not believable
tele	far away	television	the transmission of pictures far away
flect, flex	to bend	reflect	to bend back
pater	father	paternal	connected with the father
equ	even	equalize	to make even
scrib, script	to write	subscribe	to underwrite
voc, vok	to call	invoke	to call on

Practice 10

A. Building words.

1. Add a prefix to five of the following to form other words:

appear	scribe	expensive	ordinary
commend	take	marine	important
proper	arrange		

2. Add a suffix to five of the following to form other words:

begin	brother	approve	know
act	appear	disappoint	speculate
same	king		

3. Build five words with each of five of the following *prefixes:*

semi	un	pro	mis
sub	dis	mono	super
de	inter	ex	circum
anti	re	post	

4. Build five words with each of five of the following *suffixes:*

ment	ery	ness	tude
able	less	fold	fy
ism	ible	ly	ate
ity	ic	ous	

B. Use in separate sentences three of the words you formed in each of the four preceding exercises.

C. Perhaps one of the words will remind you of an experience you had. Write a short paragraph (3-5 sentences) to tell what happened. Be sure that you develop only one main idea in your paragraph.

D. Form the antonym of each of these words by adding a prefix meaning "not" or "the opposite." Then, use five of the pairs of words in sentences to illustrate their differences in meaning. For example:

> Good grades *please* my father.
> Poor grades *displease* him.

perfect	comfortable
active	religious
legal	spell
regular	intelligent
direct	kind

E. Change each of the words given below to mean "a person who" or "one who" by adding *er* or *or*. An example would be changing *dream* to *dreamer*. Notice that you will be changing words that describe an action into words that describe the actor. Notice, too, that in some cases you will find it necessary to make spelling changes.

Then, choose five of the words given and five of the new words made and write sentences to illustrate the difference in function.

sail	wait	wash	bat
fly	act	educate	paint
row	wrap	farm	operate
orate	hit	press	inspect
edit	clean	buy	win

F. Change each of the words below to mean "a person who" or "one who." You will need to use several different endings. Here, you are forming new words that are related to the words given.

Then, select five pairs of words to use in sentences that will illustrate their relationship. Thus, you might write, for *piano* and *pianist: The pianist preferred a grand piano.*

library	science	piano	pharmacy
drama	senate	grammar	biology
history	magic	music	mathematics
surgery	comedy	guitar	colony
engine	electricity	humanity	poetry

SYNONYMS, ANTONYMS, AND HOMONYMS

Sometimes a word does not carry the exact picture we may wish it to. If we say, "The soldier walked into camp," the picture is not an especially vivid one. If, on the other hand, we say, "The soldier *limped* into camp," a variety of impressions may come to mind.

Synonyms. A word that can be used for another we call a **synonym.** Notice the part of the word *syn-*, which means essentially "the same." No two words mean exactly the same, of course. But a careful use of synonyms will enliven your language and, at times, avoid a dreary overuse of the same words. A knowledge of synonyms will not only increase the extent of your vocabulary, but will also increase its precision.

Practice 11

A. Rewrite the sentences that follow, substituting more vivid or precise words for the verbs in italics.

1. The crippled old man *walked* down the street.
2. The fat lady *breathed* rapidly when she *climbed* the hill.
3. The teen-ager *honked* his horn.
4. "I'm not afraid," *said* Jim Hawkins.
5. The captain of the losing team *closed* the locker door.

B. Substitute more colorful and interesting words for the italicized words in this paragraph. You may wish to expand the paragraph as a whole.

David played a *great* game. There was a *great* crowd of people to watch him defeat the *great* opposing pitcher. He hit a *great* line drive that brought in four runs. It was a *great* day.

C. Choose different synonyms to express exactly your ideas of
color, size, manner, and mood. Match each of the following
synonyms in the right-hand column with the appropriate word in
the left-hand column.

a. dream	1. ancient, antiquated, antique
b. saw	2. devoured, gulped, swallowed
c. horn	3. tiny, miniature, puny
d. ate	4. glow, glimmer, twinkle
e. dressed	5. vision, trance, reverie
f. small	6. recent, fresh, modern
g. girl	7. lass, damsel, maiden
h. light	8. bugle, trumpet, cornet
i. old	9. spied, gazed, observed
j. new	10. robed, clad, garbed

Antonyms. You should also learn to work with **antonyms,**
words which express ideas of opposite meaning. A knowledge
of antonyms is especially helpful if you are discussing comparisons or contrasts, as in the following sentence (the antonyms are
in italics): Side by side, the two men were a startling sight, the
one so *huge* he would fill a doorway, the other so *tiny* his shoulders would barely reach the knob.

As you learned earlier in this chapter, you can also use prefixes to form antonyms, as in this sentence: The argument seemed
logical at first, but in the debate that followed, it proved to be
quite *illogical.*

If you have trouble thinking of synonyms and antonyms in
your writing, you can often find them in your dictionary. The
synonyms and antonyms for many words are listed after the
abbreviations *Syn.* and *Ant.* following the definitions.

> satisfy—to gratify to the full. Syn.—sate, suffice, surfeit.
> Ant.—disappoint, starve, stint

Practice 12

Rearrange the following list so that the words form pairs of
antonyms like *hard-soft.*

ignorant	progress	first	large
heavy	advance	quick	serious
learned	dull	retrogress	greedy
familiar	tall	straight	bright
crooked	generous	retreat	strange
last	wise	slow	short
happy	light	small	foolish

Homonyms. Also useful to a writer are words that are called **homonyms**: words that sound alike, but mean different things and contain different letters. (See pages 234–238 for further discussion of homonyms.) Here are some common homonyms:

1.	to, too, two	11.	right, write
2.	pail, pale	12.	break, brake
3.	meet, meat, mete	13.	steel, steal
4.	road, rode	14.	red, read
5.	son, sun	15.	whole, hole
6.	know, no	16.	great, grate
7.	some, sum	17.	sent, cent, scent
8.	would, wood	18.	by, buy
9.	hear, here	19.	eight, ate
10.	our, hour	20.	peace, piece

Practice 13

Select five pairs of homonyms. Write a sentence for each word of each pair to illustrate its use. Read the sentences aloud to the class. See if they can spell the words that you have used.

Points to remember

This discussion about building a vocabulary, or increasing your word power, essentially boils down to two simple methods:

Gain new word friends by exploring new subjects.

Read, read, and read some more. Study unfamiliar words you meet in your reading. Learn all you can about these words. By searching them out, draining them dry, and making the effort to put them to use, you can absorb them into your vocabulary.

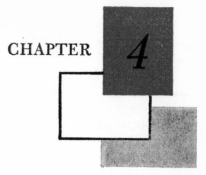

CHAPTER *4*

Effective Sentences

1. Afterward, he told his story.
2. "Listen!" the boy began.
3. "I was crouched behind the rock."
4. John told his story, while Craig listened intently.
5. "You were extremely lucky!"
6. "You might have . . ."

THE SENTENCE

Basic to all written and oral expression is the sentence. However, not every group of words we see in print is actually a sentence. Look at the six groups of words above to discover what makes one group of words a sentence and another not.

In which of the groups of words of this selection do you need more information in order to complete what the speaker started to say?

If you were reading group 6 aloud, what would happen to your voice at the end of the line? Would the pitch of your voice remain high, or would it drop?

What mark of end punctuation do you observe at the end of

groups 1, 2, and 4? What do you think this mark of punctuation indicates?

What mark of end punctuation (excluding the quotation marks) do you see at the end of groups 3 and 5? Why was this symbol used?

By comparing word groups 1 through 5 with word group 6, we can learn several important facts about the difference between groups of words that are sentences and groups of words that are not sentences.

In a complete sentence a speaker completes what he started to say in that group of words.

When you read a sentence aloud, the pitch of your voice drops at the end. We use a period to show the reader where to change the pitch of his voice. The voice pitch pattern might look like this:

High _____
                                          Low

If a group of words is not a sentence, the reader or the listener does not have the feeling that the writer or speaker has completed what he started to say, and the pitch of the voice remains high. The pattern of the voice pitch might look like this:

High _____ High

When the word group is not complete, we say that it is a **sentence fragment**. Sentence fragments can be very effective in certain kinds of writing and speaking, chiefly when we want to indicate uncertainty, surprise, or interruption. Generally, however, we write and speak in complete sentences, particularly until we have mastered the skill of writing complete sentences. Until we have mastered the use of words in conventional ways, it is wise to avoid the unconventional ways.

Study this excerpt from a story and see if you can decide which word groups are sentences and which are not.

1. In the evening the sheriff's posse arrived.
2. "Mr. Davis home?"
3. "He's in Tuscon," Martin said easily.

4. "No one else here?"
5. "The foreman . . ."
6. The sheriff scowled angrily.
7. "I've had enough from him already, mister."

In which group of words did the speaker not complete what he started to say? What mark of punctuation is used in Word Groups 2 and 4? What happens to the pitch of the voice if you read these groups aloud? What does such a word group expect of the person addressed? What does the incomplete word group indicate about Tommy?

By comparing the word groups in the above selection, we should have learned these generalizations:

1. A sentence may make a statement or ask a question.
2. A question mark is used to end a group of words that is complete but expects a reply.
3. The question mark tells the reader to raise the pitch of his voice at the end of the sentence.
4. We have learned another voice pitch pattern:

                                Higher

      High _____

5. Sentence fragments are used in certain kinds of writing to show deliberate incompleteness.

Practice 14

Read these selections softly to yourself. Decide which of the word groups are sentences. Your voice pitch pattern will help you.

I

"Now don't you see how I'm fixed? If you was to tackle this fence, and if anything was to happen . . ."

II

She looked perplexed for a moment and then said, "Well, if I get hold of you I'll . . ." (From *The Adventures of Tom Sawyer*, Mark Twain.)

III

A half-starved dog that looked like Wolf was sneaking about. Rip called him by name, but the cur snarled, showed his teeth, and passed on. This was an unkind cut indeed. "My very dog," sighed Rip, "has forgotten me." (From *The Legend of Sleepy Hollow*, by Washington Irving.)

IV

Paul: "Why so excited? Did you discover anything while I was in the hills?"

Griff: "Look at this."

Paul: "Just looks like an old piece of rag to me."

Griff: "All right, but really look at it. Smell it."

Paul: "It does smell peculiar."

Griff: "Smells like what?"

Paul: "Say, do you suppose . . ."

Griff: "Right! Kerosene!"

V

The old man shook his head solemnly. The light from the cook fire glistened on his white hair. "Tupa lives in the great caves of the reef. He is longer than this house. There is a sail on his back—not large, but terrible to see, for it burns with a white fire. Once when I was fishing beyond the reef at night, I saw him come up right under the canoe and . . ."

"What happened then?" Mako asked. (From *Call It Courage*, by Armstrong Sperry. Copyright 1940 by The Macmillan Company.)

We can summarize our observations about complete and incomplete sentences in these three statements:

1. A person who reads a sentence has a sense of completeness.

He feels at the end that the writer has finished what he started to say.

2. The sentence starts with a capital letter and ends with a period, a question mark, or exclamation mark.

3. A sentence, then, is a word group that gives the listener or reader a sense of completeness, and that contains, either expressed or implied, a verb and its subject.

Practice 15

A. Add words to these pieces of sentences to make them complete.

1. Meanwhile, back at the ranch . . .
2. In the morning, I . . .
3. From the cherry tree hung . . .
4. If I do not do my homework, my father . . .
5. When I get home after school, I . . .
6. There is no . . .
7. You know, of course, that . . .
8. The policemen stopped the motorist and . . .
9. Will you be . . .
10. Since I could not swim, I . . .

B. Answer these questions first in as few words as possible to give meaning; and then do the same thing to make complete sentences.

1. Where were you born?
2. How many brothers and sisters do you have?
3. Where do you live?
4. Do you have a pet?
5. What do you do when you are allowed to do whatever you want?

THE SIMPLE SENTENCE

You have seen that a group of words must have certain characteristics if it is to be called a sentence. Now study the italicized sentences in these selections:

I

For the first time in months Steve and I laughed and whistled and sang. We were as happy as clams. *The dark days were over. The nightmare had been lifted. That Spot was gone.* (From "That Spot," by Jack London.)

II

When Tommy opened his eyes, he was numbed with cold. He sat up dizzily. *A sharp pain shot through his left side. He shouted loudly, "Barrows! Barrows!" Only the howling of the wind answered him.* (From *Storm Flight,* by Rutherford Montgomery; copyright, 1939, by *Story Parade, Inc.* Used by permission.)

III

"I shall want your help tonight, Watson."
"At what time, Holmes?"
"Ten will be early enough."
"I shall be at Baker Street at ten."
"Very well. And, I say, Doctor, there may be some little danger, so kindly put your army revolver in your pocket. *Come promptly, Watson."* (From *Sherlock Holmes,* by Sir Arthur Conan Doyle. By permission of the Society of Authors and the Sir Arthur Conan Doyle Estates.)

In each of the italicized sentences, how many statements does the writer make?

In these italicized sentences, find sentences that make a statement, ask a question, give a command or make a request. Read these softly to yourself and notice how your voice signals the end of each sentence.

In sentences of command and request, is the subject expressed?

By studying these sentences, you can see that a sentence frequently makes only one statement, or asks only one question, or gives only one command. The writer has only one thing to say. We call such a sentence a simple sentence.

In a conversation some of the words may not be expressed.

"I shall want your help tonight, Watson."

"At what time (do you want my help), Holmes?"

We may also see that parts of the sentence are understood in a command and request.

"(You) Come promptly, Watson."

Here, *Watson* and *you* are actually the same person. *You* can be left out, since the word is understood to be said (implied).

Study the following sentences, and then answer the questions that follow.

1. The streets were very clean.
2. Men washed and polished them every morning.
3. The buildings seemed unusually bright.
4. Dad and Mother had eaten dinner.
5. I walked over and closed the door.
6. Jay stood and watched them pass in at the school house door.
7. Mother and Mrs. Stafford got up and went out.
8. The biology student held his face down and looked through the microscope.
9. We stopped and watched him.
10. I put my gym clothes away, got my books, and went down the steps.

In sentences 4 and 7, how many people are doing something?

_____ and _____ had eaten dinner.

_____ and _____ got up and went out.

In sentences 2, 5, 6, 8, 9 and 10, how many things are being done?

Men _____ and _____ them every morning.

I _____ over and _____ the door.

We _____ and _____ him.

All of the sentences we have studied here are known as simple sentences. A simple sentence may make a statement about:

> one person doing one thing,
> one person doing more than one thing,
> more than one person doing one thing, or
> more than one person doing more than one thing.

That is, a simple sentence may have more than one subject or predicate, or maybe both. But a simple sentence will not have more than one complete set of subjects and verbs functioning independently of other sets.

The simple sentence is an extremely useful device. Writers use it to express rapid action or mounting tension, or to make certain ideas stand out boldly. On the following page are some examples of the skillful use of the simple sentence:

> "I did the rest. I confess it. It was just as you say. A Stock Exchange debt had to be paid. I needed the money badly. Oberstein offered me five thousand. It was to save myself from ruin." (From *Sherlock Holmes,* by Sir Arthur Conan Doyle. By permission of the Society of Authors and the Sir Arthur Conan Doyle Estates.)

Note how the author has used the simple sentence to communicate to the reader the excitement and tension of the scene. Then, in this next passage, notice how the author creates an atmosphere of tension, again by the use of the simple sentence.

> "I held on to the rock and closed my eyes. This was the punishment of the sea. At last I took a look at what life was like. It was cheerfully normal. Wave prisms played lazily on the rocks. My companions were gone." (From *Silent World,* by Jacques Cousteau. By permission of Harper & Row, Publishers, Incorporated.)

Practice 16

A. Write five simple sentences in which one person does one thing. *(The professor adjusted the microscope.)*

B. Write five simple sentences in which more than one person does one thing. *(Jack and Jill went up the hill.)*

C. Write five simple sentences in which one person does more than one thing. *(Joe laughed, danced, and sang.)*

D. Write five simple sentences in which more than one person does more than one thing. *(Jane and Sally cooked and served a delicious dinner.)*

THE COMPOUND SENTENCE

Up to this point, you have studied only simple sentences. Sometimes, however, the simple sentence is not the most suitable way of expressing our ideas. When we express two or more closely related ideas, we may wish to use a type of sentence that expresses *both* of these ideas.

Here are some examples of sentences in which a writer is expressing two closely related ideas:

> He tried to turn his head but the obstruction prevented him.
> Alec freed the lashing, and the basket fell back into the hold.
> His hand felt the torn end of the pipe and he was free.
> A wave swung him up on the stone stairs and he plodded up to the lighthouse.
> We went back the next day to look at the mysterious road, but the barrel buoy was gone.

In each of these sentences, the author has combined two closely related ideas of equal or nearly equal importance. Although each pair of ideas could have been stated in two simple sentences, such short sentences can create a rather jerky effect when several are written one right after the other.

The kind of sentence in which we combine two or more closely related ideas that are of equal importance is called a **compound sentence.** Each of the main ideas is expressed in a group of words having a subject and a predicate. Each part of the compound sentence could function as a simple sentence, but the effect would be different.

The main ideas in a compound sentence are usually connected by conjunctions such as *and, but, or,* and *nor.* To make sure that the reader may not confuse the first idea with the one that follows, main ideas are often separated by a comma as well. In compound sentences containing ideas that are closely related, a semicolon often takes the place of the comma and the connecting word. The conjunction *but* is used most often to establish the idea of *contrast*. For a more dramatic effect, the semicolon is used, especially if the two statements are exactly similar in form.

> Jack wanted to climb the hill, but I preferred to study the sea.
>
> General Grant was practical, hard-headed, shrewd, willful; General Lee was quiet, reflective, theoretical-minded, imaginative.

Therefore, we may use a compound sentence when we wish to express in one sentence two or more ideas that we think are closely related and are of equal importance. We usually connect these ideas with words like *and, but, or,* and *for,* and we use a comma so the reader does not confuse the separate ideas.

Practice 17

A. Practice writing some compound sentences that express ideas of equal importance. On a separate sheet of paper, write your own compound sentences to fit each of the following patterns, but make sure that your ideas in each sentence are related and can be used as separate simple sentences. Notice how the connecting word *and* differs in meaning from *but.*

1. Jack _____, and Tom _____.
2. Helen _____, but Jane _____.
3. We _____, or they _____.
4. Will they _____, or should we _____?
5. We _____, and they _____.
6. Jerry _____; Jim _____.
7. _____; _____.

B. For practice in constructing simple and compound sentences, use the subjects and predicates listed below, and write ten simple sentences and ten compound sentences. Use some compound subjects and predicates in your simple sentences. You may combine the subjects and predicates in any way you wish. You may change the verbs to meet the needs of your sentences.

Subjects		Predicates	
plane	dog	soar	stand
moon	wall	fill	explain
music	circus	light	pound
carpenter	trees	howl	play
flowers	snow	run	grow
books	escape	sway	learn
stove	grass	heal	hail
chair	dew	is	fly
love	bird	stimulate	pester
car	cat	rise	chase

C. Practice recognizing simple and compound sentences. Number from 1–10 on a separate paper. Then read the following sentences. Put an S beside the numbers of the sentences that are simple sentences, and a C beside the numbers of the sentences which are compound sentences.

Beware of simple sentences with compound subjects and predicates. Remember, the compound sentence is like two simple sentences that are joined by a conjunction to indicate a close relationship between two ideas of equal importance, *or* to indicate a contrast between two ideas. Look at the following three examples. The first is a simple sentence. The next two are compound sentences.

Jack and Jim joined the football team.

Jack and Jim joined the football team, but Joe joined the swimming team.

Bill washed and ironed his own shirts, but Sam sent his shirts to the laundry.

1. Last night I arrived home without a key.
2. I tried all the doors, but they were locked.
3. The dog stood in the bedroom and wagged her tail to greet me.

4. She could not understand my unusual behavior.
5. I tried to open a window with my car key; but, alas, it did not work.
6. Finally, I happened to find a spare screwdriver in the garage.
7. I was able to pry open an unlocked window with the screwdriver, and then I carefully climbed through into the house.
8. The dog watched the whole procedure with an expression of utter amazement on her face.
9. She considered my actions highly irregular, but she forgave me nonetheless.
10. I have resolved to cache an extra key in the basement, and thus I will not have to disconcert my four-legged friend again.

THE COMPLEX SENTENCE

You have studied the simple sentence and the compound sentence. You have learned that the simple sentence expresses one main idea, although it may contain more than one subject or more than one predicate. You have also learned that the compound sentence is two or more simple sentences connected by a conjunction.

The compound sentence is used to express two or more complete ideas of equal importance. Often one of the main ideas will simply add to the information presented in the first main idea, and at other times it may contrast with the first main idea. You learned, too, that a semicolon sometimes replaces the conjunction if the ideas are closely related, or if they have exactly the same construction. Frequently, authors use this kind of sentence to present co-ordinate or parallel ideas of equal importance.

> Bill played chess.
> Bill played chess, but Joe played checkers.
> I went to Europe; John went to Asia.

Another type of sentence contains one main idea and one or

more *subordinate* ideas. A subordinate idea is one which is given less importance in the sentence than the other, or main, idea. This type of sentence is called a **complex sentence**. When you wish to express two or more related but unequal ideas, use a complex sentence.

> The tree sheltered the flowers *which grew at its base.*

The subordinate idea in this sentence is italicized. The group of words "The tree sheltered the flowers" contains the *main idea.* The other idea simply gives additional information.

The main ideas in a compound sentence are joined by conjunctions like *and, but, or,* and *for.* Subordinate ideas in complex sentences are joined to the main ideas either by words called subordinate conjunctions (words like *if, because, although, when, since,* and others), or by words called relative pronouns (*who, whose, whom, which,* and *that*).

> I left the party *although* it had barely started.
> He found the man *whose* wallet he had.
> I bought a new winter coat *because* I have outgrown my old one.

Practice 18

A. Compose six sentences in which you use the following subordinate conjunctions or relative pronouns to join subordinate ideas to main ideas.

subordinate conjunctions	relative pronouns
until	who, whose, whom
before	which
although	that

B. In the two example sentences which follow, the main idea has been separated from the subordinate idea. The subjects (S) and predicates (V) have also been indicated.

$$\overset{S}{} \qquad \overset{V}{} \qquad \overset{V}{}$$
When we presently got underway and went poking down
$$\overset{S\ \ LV}{}$$
the broad Ohio, | I became a new being.

    S   V
   Mark Twain boarded "an ancient tub called the *Paul*
       S V
Jones" | which was going to New Orleans.

Copy the sentences that follow. Underline the main idea once; underline the subordinate idea twice; mark the subjects and predicates in each one as S and V or LV.

1. I met my brother who had just returned from overseas duty.
2. The car had a tire which was flat.
3. The service station attendant who helped me knows you.
4. The kitten that we found at church has been a fine pet.
5. If you study hard, you will learn.
6. When you eat too much, you get fat.
7. She had a dress that made her look very slender.
8. Since he was in a hurry, he ran to the station.
9. Do not harm the robin that is feeding on the cherries.
10. When he felt happy, he leaped into the air.

The clause. Notice that both the cluster of words containing the main idea of the sentence and the cluster containing the subordinate idea have a subject and a predicate.

The cluster containing the main idea makes a complete thought, but the cluster containing the subordinate idea does not.

A cluster of words containing a subject and a predicate is called a **clause**. The cluster containing the main idea is called the main clause, or *independent* clause (because it can stand alone); the cluster containing the subordinate idea is called the subordinate clause, or *dependent* clause (because it depends on the main clause to give it meaning).

Practice 19

Select the main clauses and subordinate clauses in the following sentences. Copy the sentences on a separate paper. Underline the main clause once and the subordinate clauses twice. Label the subjects and predicates of each clause.

1. I stayed where the wind could strike me.
2. I experienced a joy which filled me with the purest gratitude.
3. I wished that they could see me.
4. He knew the girl who drove the red car.
5. Our dog, who insists on chasing the cat, bears many scars on his head.
6. When they did not discover me, I sneezed to get their attention.
7. I moved to a position where they could see me.
8. He wrote a letter which explained the problem.
9. Jim wondered what John intended to do.
10. When the steam cleared away, he climbed upon the boilers again.

Using subordinate clauses. A clause can function in a complex sentence as a noun, adjective, or adverb. Observe these examples:

1. I knew *what I wanted to do.*
2. He told a story *which thrilled us to the core.*
3. I swam *where the water was crystal clear.*

Example 1, patterned for S–V–O, would look like this:

S   V   O
I knew *what I wanted to do.*

Because a direct object is a noun, the subordinate clause in this sentence is functioning as a noun.

Now take a look at example 2.

He told us a story *which thrilled us to the core.*

In this sentence the subordinate clause "which thrilled us to the core" tells us something about the noun *story*. This clause *modifies* the noun *story*.

Words, phrases, or clauses that modify nouns are functioning as adjectives. Therefore, "which thrilled us to the core" is an adjective clause.

Now take a look at example 3.

I swam *where the water was crystal clear.*

The clause "where the water was crystal clear" tells where the person swam. Words, phrases, or clauses that tell where, how, or when something happened are functioning as adverbs in the sentence pattern.

Clauses that function as a particular part of speech may often be recognized by the introductory word. The following words usually introduce clauses that function as adjectives:

who	which
whose	that
whom	

Many words can be used to introduce clauses that function as nouns, including some of the words in the list above. Some of these introductory words are:

what   whoever   whomever   that

Also, many words introduce clauses that function as adverbs. Some are:

when	while
where	although
until	as
unless	as if
since	because

The important thing is to observe carefully to see how the clause is functioning. If it has one of the regular uses of a noun (subject, direct object, object of a preposition, or indirect object), it is a noun clause.

Practice 20
A. From the three lists above, select any ten words and use them to introduce subordinate clauses in ten complex sentences. Underline the main clause once and the subordinate clause twice, and tell whether the subordinate clause is functioning as a noun, an adjective, or an adverb.

B. As you have already seen, the ideas in two sentences can often be joined in a single complex sentence. Here is an example:

(two sentences)   She is the girl. She broke her leg.
(complex sentence)   She is the girl *who broke her leg.*

Here the first sentence has become the main clause, and the second sentence is now a dependent clause. Because it further identifies the girl, it is an adjective clause.

For each of the pairs of sentences which follow, write a single complex sentence. Then, in parentheses after your sentence, indicate what kind of dependent clause you have made: noun, adjective, or adverb.

1. I climbed the cherry tree. The tree stands in our garden.
2. Alice sat there by herself. The first streaks of dawn appeared.
3. I see that clock. It hangs on the wall.
4. Words stuck in Alec's throat. He looked into the eyes of his rescuers.
5. Susan brought home a turkey. It is thawing fast.
6. We thought he was calling to us. We could see his mouth move.
7. The tenor received an ovation. He sang an encore.
8. We won the game. We celebrated a victory.
9. We drove home. The game was over.
10. You win the tennis match. You will receive a trophy.
11. He lost his dog. He felt very sad.
12. She learns to sew. She has new clothes.
13. The boy broke his leg. He will not ski tomorrow.
14. The student was reading the book. He did not hear the assignment.
15. The driver did not see the stop sign. The policeman arrested him.

SUMMARY

In this chapter we have discussed three different kinds of sentences: simple, compound, and complex. The simple sentence makes a single idea stand out; the compound sentence connects two main ideas, each one of which could be written as a simple sentence; the complex sentence connects a main idea and an idea of lesser importance called a subordinate idea.

The cluster of words which contains the main idea and the cluster of words which contains the subordinate idea both contain subjects and predicates. A cluster of words which contains a subject and predicate is called a clause. There are two kinds of clauses: main, or independent, clauses; and subordinate, or dependent, clauses.

A simple sentence is one main clause.

A compound sentence is two closely related main clauses connected by a conjunction.

A complex sentence is one main clause and one subordinate clause.

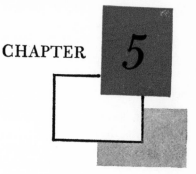

CHAPTER 5

Building Paragraphs

No matter how vivid and colorful our words and how effective and carefully formed our sentences, our writing would seldom accomplish the purpose of stating an idea fully unless we joined sentences together. Most ideas require more than just one sentence. An idea has to be developed. For this reason we learn how to put sentences together—or, perhaps it is more accurate to say that when we have an idea to express, the idea requires that we use more than one sentence to state it. This larger unit of writing is called the *paragraph*.

A paragraph is essentially a group of sentences that together develop one main idea. In a longer composition, each of the paragraphs helps to develop the topic of the whole composition by contributing a discussion about some one idea or aspect of that topic. The division of a composition into paragraphs is indicated by the fact that the first line of every paragraph is indented slightly. It is this indention that tells the reader to look for something else, a change of direction, a new idea, or a different approach to the idea that has just been written about.

Just as there is no fixed number of paragraphs that make up a composition, so there is no fixed number of sentences in a paragraph. Whether a paragraph contains one, ten, twenty, or even

more sentences is not the important thing. The important thing
is that it develops one basic or main idea.

Look at the following paragraphs from a news dispatch describing a successful manned orbital flight.

> M. Scott Carpenter became today the second American
> to orbit the earth.
>
> His three-orbit trip ended, however, with a global audi-
> ence suffering almost an hour's anxiety about his safe return.
>
> It was three hours from the time his space capsule landed
> until he was plucked from a life raft by a rescue helicopter.
> And it was hours later before the capsule was picked up by
> the destroyer *Pierce*.
>
> Coming down from orbit, the 37-year-old Navy test pilot
> was carried 250 miles beyond the intended Caribbean land-
> ing point and the remaining recovery ships. (Copyright by
> *The New York Times*. Reprinted by permission.)

You should note that each of these four short paragraphs describes one phase of the astronaut's flight, thus contributing to
the topic of the whole dispatch, the astronaut's flight. The first
paragraph makes the statement that he has made a successful
trip. The second paragraph tells the fact that everyone was wor-
ried about him. The third paragraph tells what had happened
to make people worry. The last paragraph relates the difficulties
that caused it all.

This example, however, is from a news story, a special kind of
writing in which paragraphs are unusually short and simple. In
most kinds of writing they are longer and more complex, but
every good paragraph, long or short, will still have one idea.

Very often the idea that is contained in a paragraph will be
found in what is called a *topic sentence*. Most frequently the
topic sentence is the first sentence of the paragraph, as in this
passage from Deems Taylor's *Of Men and Music*.

> *He was almost innocent of any responsibility*. Not only
> did he seem incapable of supporting himself, but it never
> occurred to him that he was ever under any obligation to

do so. He was convinced that the world owed him a living. In support of this belief, he borrowed money from everybody who was good for a loan—men, women, friends, or strangers. He wrote begging letters by the score, sometimes groveling without shame, at others loftily offering his intended benefactor the privilege of contributing to his support, and being mortally offended if the recipient declined the honor. I have found no record of his ever paying or repaying money to anyone who did not have a legal claim upon it. (From *Of Men and Music.* Copyright 1937 by Deems Taylor. By permission of Simon and Schuster, Inc.)

Notice how the paragraph develops the single idea, contained in the first, or topic sentence: "He seemed almost innocent of any responsibility." The main idea is developed in every sentence, from the second through the last, through the addition of further details. If we were to break down the idea and the supporting ideas of this paragraph, it could be outlined something like this:

    Topic: his lack of responsibility
    Developing ideas: no desire or effort to support self
                     feeling that world owed him a living
                     borrowing money from everyone
                     refusal or reluctance to repay loans

As mentioned above, the topic sentence will very frequently appear as the first sentence in the paragraph. In some paragraphs, however, the topic sentence will appear in the middle or at the end.

But, wherever the topic sentence happens to be located, the paragraph still has a topic, or main idea. Study the following paragraphs, in which the topic sentence is italicized for you.

I

You live in what is certainly an age of wonders. Manmade satellites hurtle through space at fantastic speeds. Atomic-powered submarines prowl the seven seas without refueling. Huge radio telescopes explore vast areas of the sky unknown to human vision. Electronic microscopes reveal the physical appearance of objects many times smaller than ever before perceived. (Reprinted from *All Around America*, by Robert C. Pooley, Alfred H. Grommon and Edythe Daniel; copyright © 1959 by Scott, Foresman and Company, Chicago.)

II

Or again, perhaps, you may sail for days on end without seeing anything you could recognize as life, or the indications of life, day after day of empty water and empty sky, and so you may reasonably conclude that there is no spot on earth so barren of life as the open ocean. *But if you had the opportunity to tow a fine-meshed net through the seemingly lifeless water and then to examine the washings of the net, you would find that life is scattered almost everywhere through the water like a fine dust.* A cupful of water may contain millions upon millions of tiny plant cells, each of them far too small to be seen by the human eye; or it may swarm with an infinitude of animal creatures, none larger than a dust mote, which live on plant cells smaller than themselves. (From *The Sea Around Us*, by Rachel L. Carson. Copyright 1950, 1951, © 1960 by Rachel L. Carson. Reprinted by permission of Oxford University Press, Inc.)

III

To the city dweller of today, meat is something that comes wrapped in cellophane from the supermarket, potatoes come by the pound in paper or plastic bags, and feathers grow in hats. His view of the world is quite different from that of his ancestors, who knew that meat must be hunted down in the forest, potatoes have to be planted and weeded, and only birds can produce feathers. *Yet, whether modern man realizes it or not, he is still as dependent as were his ancestors on animals and plants for his existence.* (From *Practical English*. © 1960 by Scholastic Magazines, Inc. Reprinted by permission.)

A writer places his topic sentence, if he has one, in the position that best achieves the effect he desires. In expository writing, in which he is explaining or describing something, the topic sentence is very likely to appear first. Thus, the reader knows what the writing is about, and the details that follow develop that main idea.

If the topic sentence comes last, the chances are that the writer has wished to build up to a climax. Notice the rather dramatic effect of placing the topic sentence last in the final example given above. Everything builds up to the main idea in a strong fashion.

Practice 21

A. Read each of the following paragraphs. On a separate sheet of paper, write a one-sentence summary of the *main idea*. Then, seek out the topic sentence, if there is one, and write it down next to the summary you have just given. You may find that your summary and the topic sentence are nearly identical.

1. The goal tender in ice hockey is more than just another player—one, perhaps, who skates less well than others. He needs to see the pattern of the opponent's play and to relay that information to his teammates. He frequently needs to make quick decisions, especially when forwarding a trapped puck to the right place. And, of course, he needs to have the reflexes of a cat and the obstinacy of a mule to keep the opponents from scoring on him.

2. Jeff's story reads like a travel folder. He was born in Davenport, Iowa, and has at one time or another lived in Moline, Rockford, and Chicago (all in Illinois), before moving to Kenosha, Wisconsin. He lived in Kenosha long enough to attend Mary D. Bradford High School, where he starred in football, basketball, and track. (From *Practical English.* © 1961 by Scholastic Magazines, Inc. Reprinted by permission.)

3. You soon come to disregard rain on such excursions, at least in the summer, it is so easy to dry yourself, supposing a dry change of clothing is not to be had. You can much sooner dry you by such a fire as you can make in the woods than in anybody's kitchen, the fireplace is so much larger, and wood so much more abundant. A shed-shaped tent will catch and reflect the heat like a Yankee-baker, and you may be drying while you are sleeping. (From *The Maine Woods,* by Henry Thoreau.)

4. The problem of royal education is certainly difficult. How can a child grow into a normal adult if the national anthem is played on his birthday and headlines announce every stage of his progress with more emphasis than they give to the deaths of a thousand people in a battle or a famine? How is he to grow up in a sensible relation with other boys if his first jolly experience of kicking a football is photographed on ten million newspaper pages? (From *The Magic of the British Monarchy,* © Kingsley Martin 1962, reprinted with the permission of Atlantic-Little, Brown and Company, Publishers, and David Higham Associates, Ltd.)

B. Select one of the following topic sentences and write a paragraph that develops it. You may wish to begin by following the outline suggested on page 69, in which you list several ideas that support the main idea. Notice, also, that your topic sentence need not come first, although it is easier to place it there. You will probably want to modify the sentence given to fit your own style of writing.

1. If you are in trouble while swimming, the important thing to remember is not to panic.
2. It is easy to see how means of transportation have improved in the last fifty years.
3. Keeping our highways attractive has become a problem.
4. It is not always easy to live up to our parents' expectations of us.

PLANNING

You have seen how the authors of the foregoing paragraphs have developed their topic sentences by giving supporting details and examples. It is important in writing a paragraph that the sentences relate to the main idea. Thus, if you are writing a paragraph on your favorite summer sports, skiing would probably not be related to the main idea unless you were trying to show a contrast.

To be sure that supporting sentences relate to the main idea, it is advisable to have a plan in mind. You need to think ahead if you are to express yourself clearly. Any such plan is really an outline of what you are going to say. It does not need to be elaborate. Even the simplest outline, such as the one on page 69, will help you organize and unify what you write.

To aid in your planning of a paragraph, remember some of the points that are characteristic of any good piece of writing, whether it is just a sentence, a paragraph, or a longer composition.

Originality. Good writing will always reflect the originality and even the personality of the writer. When you write, you express your own ideas. The person who reads what you have written is seeing something of your personality.

Accuracy. Your writing must not only be accurate in content, but also accurate in its presentation.

Clarity. An accurate presentation of material in a paragraph will depend to a large extent on the clarity with which it is presented. The use of precise words, straightforward style, and a sure focus on the topic are all a part of clarity.

Conciseness. Unnecessary words can obscure the meaning of writing probably more quickly than any other single fault. Nor is it necessary to repeat an idea three or four times to make it stick. A brief statement of your topic and the developing ideas is enough.

Unity, Coherence, and Emphasis. It is important that your writing develop exactly those ideas it sets out to develop, that it proceed from point to point in a logical and orderly manner, with clear transitions between one point and another. The most important points should be emphasized in some way, either by using especially strong phrases or by placing them in a part of the paragraph, such as the beginning or end, where they will stand out.

It is a good idea when you have finished a piece of writing to ask yourself whether it measures up to these standards. Each one, as you will have already understood, depends to a great extent on the others. Thus, it would be difficult to be accurate without being coherent and clear, just as it would be hard to be clear without being concise.

Thus far, we have studied the development of the main idea in a paragraph by the addition of details that support or explain the main idea. Let us turn now to the ways in which we can develop those details that are so important in writing a paragraph.

Kinds of paragraph development.   In this discussion, we shall disregard three kinds of paragraphs: (1) the news story, which is often so broken up for quick and easy reading that it does not follow a logical form; (2) the narrative paragraph, which follows no set rules, but depends on the way the story is being told; and (3) the descriptive paragraph, which is discussed in the chapter on storytelling.

Our study of the formal paragraph here applies mainly to *exposition* and *persuasion*. In these kinds of writing, you are explaining or clarifying ideas or processes, or you are trying to win others to your point of view.

There are five principal ways of developing an expository or persuasive paragraph:

1.)   by particular facts or details
2.)   by illustration or example
3.)   by classification
4.)   by definition
5.)   by comparison and contrast

Particular facts and details.   Look first at the paragraph that follows:

Bernard de Menthon, the holy man, had long dreamed of building a monastery just there. And paying no heed to those who would discourage him, he went ahead with his work. Woodcutters felled trees in the forests below the timberline; carters with their sturdy donkeys dragged the logs up the mountainside; carpenters shaped the lumber and put it into place. At last, in the year 962, the monastery was completed. (From *Each In His Own Way*, by Alice Gall and Fleming Crew. Reprinted by permission of Henry Z. Walck, Inc.)

A brief outline of the topic and supporting details of this paragraph would look something like this:

Topic: Bernard went ahead with his dream of building a monastery.

Developing ideas: woodcutters felled the trees,
carters dragged the logs up the mountainside,
carpenters cut the lumber and placed it.

In such a paragraph as this, the order is the natural and useful one of stating the main idea and then taking up, one by one, the details that develop it. Here the details have a chronological order; that is, they are treated in the order in which they happened. We call this *time* sequence. In other cases it might be more natural to handle details in the order of their growing or decreasing *importance*, or in some other natural order. Such an order might be *space* sequence in which we show the relation of objects to one another in a given area, or in a location.

Practice 22

A. Read the following paragraph and note afterward, on a sheet of paper, the main idea and the details that support it.

As usual, Tad became his father's shadow. Wherever the President was, there—if possible—was Tad. Again and again the boy would run in from play, fling himself on his father for a quick hug, and then rush out of the room like a whirlwind. If Lincoln's office door was shut, Tad would give his special signal, three sharp raps and two slow thumps, and the door was opened no matter how many important visitors the President might have. (From *Abraham Lincoln,* by Enid LaMonte Meadowcroft. Copyright 1942 by the publishers, Thomas Y. Crowell Company, New York.)

B. Select one of the following topics, or situations, about which to write a paragraph. Think through your topic first, perhaps using the form suggested for you. When you have finished, use the check list provided on pages 67–68 to make sure your writing is clear, concise, accurate, unified, and above all original.

1. Being the oldest (youngest) in the family has its advantages (disadvantages).
2. Homework should (should not) be given regularly.
3. Our dog does not like strangers or deliverymen.
4. City life (country life) has its advantages.
5. I would rather be (right-handed) (left-handed).

Illustration and example. A second way to develop a paragraph is by illustration—that is, by telling a little story or by giving one or more examples to dramatize or illustrate the point to be made in the paragraph. Here we are obviously still using details, but the details are included as part of the illustrative story. Sometimes such a story is so strong, with so clear a meaning, that the idea it illustrates never needs to be actually stated. The parable, which the teachers of ancient times used to express a moral lesson, is an example of such a story. No moral is actually stated; the hearer simply draws his own conclusions from the words and deeds of the characters. Thus, the story itself made the point.

Look at the following paragraph, in which examples are used to develop the main idea.

From first to last, the Civil War armies enlisted no men as cooks, and there were no cooks' and bakers' schools to help matters. Often enough, when in camp, a company would simply be issued a quantity of provisions—flour, pork, beans, potatoes, and so on—and invited to prepare the stuff as best it could. Half a dozen men would form a mess, members would take turns with the cooking, and everybody had to eat what these amateurs prepared or go hungry. Later in the war, each company commander would usually detail two men to act as cooks for the company, and if either of the two happened to know anything about cooking the company was in luck. One army legend held that company officers usually detailed the least valuable soldiers to this job, on the theory that they would do less harm in the cook shack than anywhere else. One soldier, writing after the war, asserted flatly: "A company cook is a most peculiar being; he generally knows less about cooking than any other man in the company. Not being able to learn the drill, and too dirty to appear on inspection, he is sent to the cook house to get him out of the ranks." (Bruce Catton, "Hayfoot, Strawfoot!" *American Heritage,* Vol. VIII, No. 3, April, 1957.)

The central idea of this paragraph, the unorganized way in which the Civil War armies were fed, is developed by fact and illustration. The facts detailed are further developed by the anecdotes told at the end.

The point is, when developing expository paragraphs by illustration or example, you do not simply tell stories; you tell stories to prove or illustrate something.

Practice 23

A. Write a paragraph in which you develop the main idea by illustration. Here are some suggested topics.

1. Pride certainly goes before a fall.
2. Sometimes a party, which is supposed to be fun, is pure agony.
3. No man can understand the system that women drivers use.
4. The weather of _____ is the most unpredictable in the world.

B. Write a paragraph in which you support the main idea through details of a personal experience you have had. Notice, and this is important, that a personal experience need not be as dramatic as the climbing of Mt. Everest or skin-diving off the coast of France to be worth writing about. An incident that happened to you in school, in a supermarket, at home, or anywhere is quite likely to be of considerable interest.

Begin with a topic sentence—after you have a topic, of course—and then develop it, as the sample paragraphs have been developed, with details of your experience that will support your main idea.

Dividing and classifying. Sometimes, when we are explaining some technical process or a complicated method of doing something, it is convenient to divide the subject into its separate parts and handle them one at a time. Or we may classify the kinds of things included in the topic, much as we have classified the different kinds of paragraphs in this chapter.

Such a method is more easily applied to broad topics than to smaller ones. In developing a single paragraph, it may not be as vivid as using illustration or example; on the other hand, it may be much clearer and more precise.

Notice how the following paragraph divides and subdivides the topic.

> Lumber, which is still commercially important in spite of the growing use of synthetic materials, comes from two great classes of tree: the softwoods (or *conifers*) and the hardwoods (or *dicotyledons*). The softwoods include the familiar and useful evergreens, such as pine, fir, cypress, some cedar, and, of course, the giant California redwood. From the hardwoods we get an even greater variety: ash, beech, hickory, elm, oak, maple, walnut, sycamore, eucalyptus, teak, and various kinds of mahogany, from all of which huge quantities of valuable wood are obtained each year.

Having made this classification, the author is now ready to discuss each of the tribes in a separate paragraph or in groups of paragraphs.

Practice 24

Write a paragraph in which you describe some operation or process by dividing it into its parts. Be sure to include every important detail. Remember that this method has one basic purpose: to make something that is difficult or new clear to someone else.

Definition.   Sometimes, in writing and speaking, we find that it is necessary to define our terms, to make clear what it is we mean when we use a particular word. What do we mean by *patriotic?* By *good?* If we are praising *school spirit,* do we mean by this phrase support of a team, obedience to rules, care of buildings and equipment, or willingness to take part in school activities?

To define means to limit. To this extent, all paragraphs contain some definition, for they necessarily limit the topic. But there are paragraphs in which we set out especially to define a position or idea, just as Abraham Lincoln did in the following speech when he first ran for office in 1832:

> Fellow citizens: I presume you all know who I am. I am humble Abraham Lincoln. I have been solicited by many friends to become a candidate for the legislature. My politics are short and sweet, like the old woman's dance. I am in favor of a national bank. I am in favor of the internal improvement system, and a high protective tariff. These are my sentiments and political principles. If elected, I shall be thankful; if not it will be all the same.

Practice 25

Write a paragraph in which you define one of the following terms, or another term of your own choosing. Use any method or combination of methods that seems appropriate: details, illustration, or direct definition. Do not, however, begin with a dictionary definition.

1. True Friendship
2. The American Way

3. Snobbery
4. The Ideal Teacher
5. Honor

Comparison and contrast. One of the surest ways to get a clear look at something is to hold it up against something else very much like it, and then observe how it is different. Another way is to hold it up against something very different and see in what ways it is similar. Comparing things that are too much alike or too different does little good, however. One Jonathan apple is too much like another to tell us anything. But a Jonathan apple may be contrasted effectively with a Golden Delicious. Although they have much in common, they are different in color, flavor, and shape. Similarly, we may compare the atom with the solar system because, despite the enormous difference in their sizes, they are similar in their structure and motion.

In the following example, the writer contrasts the actual with the imagined in discussing a typical attitude.

> Many people seem to have an unaccountable yearning for what they call the "good old days." Apparently, they prefer to ride in a wagon that gets stuck in mudholes, loses wheels, and lets in the rain, than in an automobile that takes you where you want to go in a matter of a very few, dry minutes. Instead of turning the switch to light a lamp, heat the stove, or turn on the furnace, they'd be happier straining their eyes with candles, rekindling the fire in the old wood burner three times a day, or spending the winter shoveling coal in the cellar. Well, they can have it. I like my comforts of home.

Practice 26

Frequently, a paragraph such as the preceding sample is part of a longer composition, and one point of view is presented in one paragraph and the second point of view in the following paragraph.

Write two paragraphs, using the subject expressed in the sample paragraph just given. In one paragraph, list several things we take for granted in our modern world. Then, in the other paragraph, list details that contrast with the details in your first paragraph. You will probably want to list more items than were mentioned in the sample paragraph. It is very likely that you can get help from your parents, grandparents, or other older people that you know.

QUESTIONS TO ASK YOURSELF

Writing paragraphs, as you will see, is not an end in itself. While there are many times in which a single paragraph will express all that you wish to say, the chances are that your paragraphs will each be a part of a larger unit, containing a number of paragraphs. In the next chapter, we will discuss putting paragraphs together to make a longer composition.

In writing paragraphs, however, as in writing single sentences or whole compositions, the same care is required. As you write each piece, be sure you have followed the points listed on pages 67 to 68. In addition, here are some further points you should be aware of in all your writing:

1. Is your topic clear to you, and have you expressed it clearly to your reader? Furthermore, is your topic worth discussing?

2. Have you expressed yourself in details that are not only clear and to the point, but that are also forceful, interesting, and vivid?

3. Is your opening sentence, whether or not a topic sentence, going to arouse the reader's interest? Does your ending bring everything in your piece to a reasonable and convincing close?

4. Are your mechanics of expression as correct as you know how to make them? Check your spelling, punctuation, grammar, and sentence construction.

5. Most important, have you thought your topic through, properly organizing and planning the writing of it? Does it follow a logical order?

6. Have you revised it?

CHAPTER 6

Putting Paragraphs Together

In the two previous chapters you have learned how to write effective sentences and how to put them together into effective paragraphs. Both the sentence and the paragraph, however, are only parts of what we think of as the longer composition.

In some ways it is easier to write a composition of several paragraphs than it is to write just one paragraph. Writing a single paragraph on a good topic can prove difficult, because you may very well have too much to say for such a brief paper. As we have said, there is no precise or particular length that a composition ought to be. However, in your beginning work in putting paragraphs together to form the "whole" composition, you will probably do well to keep your paper fairly short. Unless an idea is especially worthy of a long discussion, it is better to limit yourself to five or six well-constructed paragraphs.

How do you start a composition? Actually, the process is the same as for writing a single paragraph. To begin with, you must have an over-all idea, and you must have thought it over. Before you write anything, you should have a good idea of what you intend to say about it.

PLANNING THE COMPOSITION

Planning a composition will be much easier for you if you learn right from the start how to outline your ideas. Just as you planned the paragraph, so you plan the longer composition by starting with a topic and following it with details that support it.

Let us examine a topic which might be expanded into an outline for a composition.

Topic: The advantages of a high school education

Our next step is to consider what actually are the advantages of a high school education. Most people will very likely think immediately of two very important and practical answers:

A. The increased opportunities for better jobs
B. The chance for a higher, or college, education

A little further thought, however, should turn up some other reasons, perhaps harder to define, but important just the same. As an example, in most areas of the country, people become eligible to take an active part in our democratic type of government soon after leaving high school. Therefore, we might add another statement:

C. The preparation to be a good citizen

What does all we have said thus far add up to? If we have better jobs, perhaps a college education, and the ability to act—wisely, we hope—in governmental affairs, is there nothing else? With some further reflection many people would agree that there is something else:

D. The chance to lead a more satisfactory personal life

Our outline has now grown to look something like this:

Topic: The advantages of a high school education
A. The increased opportunities for better jobs
B. The chance for higher education
C. The preparation to be a good citizen
D. The chance to live a more satisfactory life

So far so good. If you look back to the preceding chapter on building paragraphs, you can see that the plan as used here resembles those plans suggested for a single paragraph. Actually, a paragraph could be constructed from this plan alone, but it is probably safe to say that it will not be very satisfactory. There is too much that can be said about the topic to put into a single paragraph without making it too long and too packed with ideas.

Therefore, we can perhaps solve the problem by treating each of the developing details as if it were a paragraph and needed its own details to develop it.

A. The increased opportunities for better jobs

If we were writing a paragraph, what might we say about this idea, keeping in mind, of course, that we are discussing it from the point of view of a high school education? First of all, it is a safe assumption that, in today's world, the high school diploma carries a certain amount of weight just by itself. All other things being the same, employers are more likely to hire someone with a diploma than they are someone without one. Just the fact that a student has "seen it through" is often evidence enough of some satisfactory prospects for the future.

Second, the general training a student receives is likely to qualify him more than the person who has not had a high school education. At least we can assume he has been exposed to more training. His English should be better, his mathematics should be better, and he may well have had specific training, perhaps in business courses or in distributive education, that gives him added qualifications.

Finally, his outlook on life in general is likely to be better, and certainly the prospective employer will be likely to think so. The boy or girl who has completed high school has, as we mentioned above, at least "seen it through," and as a result, his general knowledge and point of view should be that much more mature.

Thus, we have these things to list under the first subtopic of the outline below and on the next page:

A. The increased opportunities for better jobs

1. Employers prefer a student with a high school diploma.
2. His special education will very likely be greater than that of a non-high school graduate.
3. His all-around development and knowledge will be greater, and the fact that he has "seen it through" will be in his favor.

There are probably many more reasons one could give in support of this particular developmental detail. There will be reasons that are similar to these, and some which may apply more in your own case than in others. But these are three basic reasons why job-seeking will be easier for the high school graduate.

Practice 27

Complete the example outline, filling in the details that you feel should develop the other three headings:

B. The chance for a higher education
C. The preparation to be a good citizen
D. The chance to live a more satisfactory life

Now, write a composition of your own anywhere from four to six paragraphs in length. As a first possible topic, write the composition for which we have just detailed the outline. Or, if you prefer another topic, perhaps one of the following will be more usable for you:

1. The school years should be shorter (or longer!).
2. How I prepare for an evening of doing homework.
3. How to impress the teacher.

Before leaving the subject of outlining, there are several things to be noted. First, there is more than one accepted way of drawing up an outline. The method we have used here is that of placing a major heading beneath the topic and placing subheadings beneath the major heading. The outline form looks something like this:

The Topic
A. (a major heading, or idea about the topic)
   1.

    2. (details that develop the first major heading)
    3.
B.
    1.
    2. (details that develop the second major heading)
    3.
C.
    1.
    2. (details that develop the third major heading)
    3.

Sometimes a topic may be easily subdivided into two or three major subtopics. Perhaps for the topic "The advantages of a high school education," we might want to list such subtopics as "more immediate practical reasons for obtaining a high school education" and "long-range goals of a high school education." In this case, we would use Roman numerals for our principal subdivisions.

Topic
The advantages of a high school education
Subtopic
I. The immediate practical advantages of a high school education
Major headings
  A. The increased opportunities for a better job
    1. (details)
    2. (details)
    3. (details)
  B. The chance for a higher education
    1. (details)
    2. (details)
    3. (details)
Subtopic
II. The long-range goals of a high school education
Major headings
  A. The preparation to be a good citizen
    1. (details)

      2. (details)
      3. (details)
   B. The chance to live a more satisfactory life
      1. (details)
      2. (details)
      3. (details)

The method we have been studying here is a standard topical outline method. Other ways of doing the outline will very often appear to be more practical than a detailed outline such as we have just discussed. A frequently used method is that of the sentence outline, in which the writer merely writes sentences, one after the other, that give a sense of the way he would like his paper to develop.

Finally, a word of caution about outlines. People sometimes arrive at the conclusion that the outline is the most important thing. Having once written an outline, they dare not change an idea or the order of ideas. If you remember that an outline is simply an aid to thinking, then it will be apparent to you that changing an outline is just another step in the thinking process. There are, in fact, writers who use an outline to check the logic of their thinking—who write the outline *after* the first draft, but before the second.

Practice 28

Choose one of the following topics, or one of your own. Without doing any further research, draw up an outline of the things you feel ought to be included in a composition on that particular topic.

Then, when you have made your outline, put it aside and do some careful thinking about the topic. Then, write another outline and compare it with your original version. Notice how the second outline has gained strength from your more careful planning.

1. Billboards along the highways are undesirable (or desirable).
2. Everyone should have a hobby.

3. Watching television programs is a harmful (useful) way to pass the time.

ORGANIZING

The outline is a method of choosing and organizing the ideas and details that go into a composition. The next step is to examine ways of making these ideas and details fit together in an orderly way.

In many compositions the order of details and ideas will be suggested quite naturally by the topic. Such was the case in the sample composition we have been outlining, the advantages of a high school education. The decision, once the ideas are selected, is simply to determine which of the major topics to put first, and which topics should come next. The desirable order in any composition is one in which the details lead naturally from one to the next.

There are several possible orders you might choose. One is the *order of importance,* in which the details run in sequence from the most important to the least important, or, in reverse, from the least important to the most important. Another order is that of time sequence. Such an organization is known as a *chronological* order. Whatever order you choose, the important thing is to get a useful relationship of ideas.

Ideas must fit together, one leading naturally to the next. One of the most common types of writing is the "how to" paper, in which the relationship of ideas is quite obviously important. An example of "how to" writing follows.

How to Handle the Message

When a message is handed into your radio station, you should be careful to check the following items. Read the message and be sure it is legible. See that all the information as to who is sending it, the organization and the person, is included on the message blank or sheet of paper on which it is written. Enter the hour and minute at which you accept it. All these things should be done before the person leaves the station. Then give the message the proper serial number, the call letter of the station, and at the right of the call letter, the personal signature of the signaler who will handle the message if you are to use it. Again, at the right of the personal signature, enter the letters "CK" (the abbreviation for "check") followed by the number of words in the message, and finally the message itself. (From the *Boy Scout Handbook*.)

Here the details have been arranged in a list form. Notice, also, that there is a time element in the order of details. Time sequence can be especially important when explaining how to do something.

Practice 29

A. In the following recipe from a newspaper, explaining how to cook soft-shelled crabs, the order of paragraphs is incorrect. Rearrange the paragraphs in what you consider to be the proper order, and then answer the questions that follow.

Curried Soft-shell Crabs

Mix some almonds with heavy cream and add to the sauce and bring to a boil. Add salt and pepper to taste. Remove from the heat.

Dip the crabs in flour and brown quickly in butter. Add them to the sauce and let them cook for ten minutes. Serve with rice.

To make the sauce, sauté two onions in five tablespoons of butter until they are golden. Add apples and tomatoes. Cover and simmer for one hour. Put through a coarse sieve. Add curry powder and 1 cup of white wine. Return to the stove and cook for ten minutes. Yield: six servings.

1. Explain why the order first given was not correct.
2. What else would you have to know to follow this recipe? That is, what knowledge on your part does the recipe assume?

B. Assume you are explaining the proper way to boil an egg to a Martian. He has never seen an egg, a stove, or even a pot of water. Explain, in as complete detail as you think necessary, the proper way to perform this simple procedure.

WRITING AND REWRITING

You have now learned something about planning the details of a composition and about planning the order in which the details should go. The next step is that of actually writing the composition; you now put your ideas on paper in a logical and sequential form.

However, a mistake that many people make is to consider the first writing of a paper as the final, finished product. Actually, there is another and vitally important step to be taken before any paper is properly considered finished.

The first writing of a paper is called the *first draft*. In the first draft, you are writing down the results of your hard work, thinking out and planning your paper. Actually, it is only now that you are ready for the final step of recopying your work into its final form. In this step, you recopy the *revised* form of your first draft. Almost any professional writer expects to make several drafts before he considers his job done.

Revising means several things. It means, first of all, looking through your paper for all the mistakes in spelling, punctuation, and grammar that you can find, and correcting them. You will not always find all of them, but you should find the most obvious ones and correct them.

Second, revising means checking through to find whether you have said what you want to say in the way you planned to say it. Is the style right? Do your sentences carry the message? Is the order of details right? If your composition has been assigned for homework, it is sometimes a good idea to read the paper aloud to yourself before taking it to school. Often you will hear something that you didn't notice when just reading it.

Of course, many papers will be written and revised during class time. If you are assigned a paper in class, it is wise to leave a bit of time for going through it to make such corrections as you wish. In such cases you probably won't rewrite. Therefore, your corrections should be made as neatly as possible by crossing out the error with a single solid line and writing the revised version over it.

Practice 30

Your teacher will return to you one of the compositions that you wrote earlier this year. With the experience you have now had in planning and writing a composition, you should be able to see more clearly some of the errors of style, grammar, and thought that you made on the earlier paper.

Revise this paper, making your corrections right on the paper itself. Then, rewrite the paper in its revised form.

STEPS TO FOLLOW

In all writing, especially in that done in a limited time, such as in class, the importance of preplanning should be very clear. In your writing, try to follow a plan of work such as this:

1. Plan—and *think*, using an outline as an aid.
2. Write.
3. Read through, correct, and rewrite.
4. Reread and copy over (if you have the time).

In doing your rereading and revision, whether in class or at home, you should find the following check list valuable:

   I. The thought of the composition

      A. Do I state my ideas clearly?
      B. Do I develop the main idea sufficiently?
      C. Do I show how less important ideas are related to it?
      D. Will the reader be able to discover easily what my composition is about?

  II. Organization
      A. Have I followed my outline?

B. Does my composition have a good beginning and a good ending?

C. Does each point follow logically from the one that went before it?

D. Does each paragraph develop one main idea?

E. Are my sentences well constructed?

    1. Are they all complete?

    2. Is there variety?

III. Choice of words

A. Have I used an interesting and suitable vocabulary?

B. Have I used colorful, forceful, and effective words?

C. Have I avoided worn-out phrases?

IV. Mechanics

A. Have I spelled as well as I can? (Look up those words you are not sure about.)

B. Are my grammar and usage correct? (The chapters on words and sentences will help you here.)

C. Is my punctuation correct? (The chapter on punctuation will help you here.)

Practice 31

A. Choose one of the following topics on which to write a three- to five-paragraph composition. Outline and organize your paper, write it, revise it, and then rewrite it.

1. Junior high schools should (or should not) have a full program of tackle football.
2. The dos and don'ts of bicycle riding.
3. A topic of your own on which you have some strong opinions.

B. You have been selected to explain to a group of visiting parents what your class has been doing this year in social studies. Divide your topic accordingly into two, three, or more headings, fill in the details, and write out the discussion as you would wish to present it.

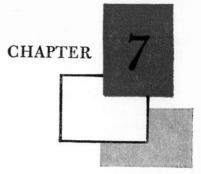

CHAPTER 7

Storytelling

It is difficult for people to converse at all without telling a story. Some people are good storytellers and others are not. Some can hold their listeners to the last word; others find their listeners yawning or drifting away to other conversations.

One magazine, *The New Yorker,* has a regular "department" called "Letters We Never Finished Reading." It consists simply of the beginnings of letters, beginnings that make the reader want to go no further. In the same way, all of us could with little trouble make up a list of stories to which we never finished listening. How many times has someone insisted on telling you the plot of a movie he has just seen?

> There's this beachcomber—he's sort of the beatnik type—and he's just sort of living around on the beach of this island, and this ship comes in—there's a storm, and everything blows down, palm trees and grass huts flying through the air—and the ship runs aground on this reef and everybody gets drowned but this girl. So you know the old routine. The beatnik is out wandering around in the wind and rain, when here comes this girl on a big wave, hanging onto a piece of two-by-four or something . . .

And on he goes. Or perhaps you've heard the girl who is always telling you "What I Did Yesterday."

> Yesterday the goofiest thing happened to me in study hall. I was in the back row—I started in the front, but Miss Breen moved me back because I whispered too much. Naturally I wouldn't have whispered if she hadn't made me change seats just before that to the one next to Abbie Saver. She put me first beside Peter Snedley, and you know how I dislike *him*. Well, I made a face at him because he said something smart, and . . .

No professional short-story writer or novelist would ever tell a story in either of these ways. He couldn't afford to; no one would read his works. Actually, though, both the movie-plot teller and the what-happened-to-me-yesterday girl have used some of the elements of sound storytelling. The first has some idea of how to be vivid, and the second knows that stories are about people and that people can be interesting. But there is more to good storytelling.

The art of storytelling has been developed over many centuries, for the story is not only the most popular form of literature, but probably the oldest. Stories were undoubtedly told orally long before the invention of writing. In ancient times, all the history and past of a people, its legends and myths, were passed on from generation to generation in story form. And passed on with the stories was the art of telling them.

Surprise is not part of traditional oral storytelling. Instead, the storyteller tells a well-known story in an interesting way; he uses his voice well or he uses special gestures to hold his listeners' attention. Very often, too, such traditional stories are really what were described on pages 70 to 71 under "Illustration and Example"; they point out a moral of some sort.

Following is one of the earliest of these traditional stories to be written down. It comes to us from Aesop, a Greek slave who lived nearly 3,000 years ago. His stories, called "fables," involve animals that talk and act like human beings. The words and actions of these animal characters are used to point a moral for human beings. The fable always has two parts: the story and the moral. The moral may not be expressed, but it must always be understood. Here, of course, it is stated for you.

The Tortoise and the Eagle

A tortoise became dissatisfied with his lowly life when he saw so many birds enjoying themselves in the air.

"If I could only get up into the air, I could soar with the best of them," he thought.

One day an eagle came to rest on a rock beside him, and, seizing such a favorable opportunity, the tortoise offered him all the treasures of the sea if only the monarch of the air would teach him to fly.

The eagle at first declined the task, for he considered it not only absurd but impossible, but being further pressed by the entreaties and the promises of the tortoise, he at length consented to do his best.

Taking him to a great height in the air, he loosed his hold, bidding the silly creature fly if he could.

Before the tortoise could express a word of thanks, he fell upon a huge rock and was dashed to pieces.

Moral: *The over-ambitious often destroy themselves.*

Notice that this story begins with a **situation,** in this case a problem which has to be solved. The tortoise is driven by his foolish desire to fly and will not rest until he gets his wish.

From this situation, the story proceeds through a series of events. The eagle appears. The tortoise makes his request, which the eagle at first refuses, and then consents to carry out. These events are called the **complication.** The final event in the complication is the point at which the eagle releases the tortoise, telling him to fly if he can. This final event, where the story reaches its highest point, is called the **climax.** Here the problem has been solved, in one way or another.

Usually a story winds up very quickly after the climax. In this case there is only one further sentence. There is nothing more to tell, and the author concludes his story as simply as possible.

The entire series of events from the situation through the climax and ending is known as the **plot** of a story. A plot is simply what happened in the story, told in the proper order of happening. Most stories include many more details than does the one just related, details of scene and details of character. The fable uses only a plot so simple that it is almost in skeleton form. Some modern stories, on the other hand, have plots that are quite difficult to follow.

Practice 32

A. Restate the moral of "The Tortoise and the Eagle" in your own words. Write a story of your own demonstrating the truth of this moral.

B. Write a fable of your own, remembering that fables are usually about animals that act and talk like human beings, that they are very short, and that they state or suggest a moral. Often, too, they are humorous and make fun of some sort of human foolishness.

ELEMENTS OF STORYTELLING

Only when telling jokes or fables are modern storytellers likely to deal in bare plots. Modern stories are nearly always much longer and more detailed. Most of them say much more about people, the characters. Most stories also try to say something about some problem in modern life. Often, too, today's story does not reveal its meaning as readily as the traditional story does. It tries to persuade the reader to live the action so vividly that he will see the meaning for himself without having to be told. Today's story wants to give the reader a sharp and vivid experience, to hold his attention to the end, to scare him or coax him into feeling that the experience of the story might actually have happened to him.

Thus, a writer must create people, places, and actions very clearly and vividly. If *what happens* is most important, the writer must pay most of his attention to plot: the situation, complications, and climax. If *how* or *why a thing happens* is most important, and the writer is more interested in *why* people do things than in *what* they do, he must be especially concerned about making the people or characters seem real. Then, since many modern stories try to create life as it really is, writers devote a great deal of effort to showing us the real world, its scenes and places, it sounds and smells, and the way it looks or feels.

Everyone understands a little how these things are done, even our movie reporter and our girl from study hall. But, since storytelling is an art, and a complicated one, learning how to practice it well takes some studying. There are a few basic things that will help you start.

Stories exist in time. Stories happen as life happens. One thing comes after another, and the order is important. It is important, for example, whether a man beats his wife *before* she puts a spider in his coffee, or afterward.

Until you have had practice trying out other ways, it is best to use the normal order of time, that is, from the first event to the last.

Perhaps the most important thing about time is that it must be constantly shown to the reader. Even in the simplest story, phrases such as *when, as soon as, then, shortly, by morning,* and *the next day* are useful and necessary. Look at the paragraph below, in which the time words and phrases have been italicized. Although it is a descriptive passage, and time is not very important, there are several clear indications of time.

> It was at Warm Springs in the Little Antelope I came upon her *in the heart of a clear forenoon*. The spring lies off a mile from the main trail, and has the only trees about it known in that country. *First* you come upon a pool of waste full of weeds of a poisonous dark green, every reed ringed about the water-level with a muddy white incrustation. *Then* the three oaks appear staggering on the slope, and the spring sobs and blubbers below them in ashy-colored mud. All the hills of that country have the down plunge toward the desert and back abruptly toward the Sierra. The grass is thick and brittle and bleached straw-colored toward the end

of the season. *As I rode* up the swale of the spring I saw the Walking Woman sitting where the grass was deepest, with her black bag and blanket, which she carried on a stick, beside her. *It was one of those days when* the genius of talk flows as smoothly as the rivers of mirage through the blue hot desert morning. (From "The Walking Woman," in *Lost Borders* by Mary Austin, Harper & Brothers, 1909. Copyright, 1909, by Harper & Brothers. Copyright, 1936, by the Estate of Mary Austin. Reprinted by permission of Harper & Row and the Estate of Mary Austin.)

In a story where the order and timing of events is more important, time phrases are likely to occur with great frequency.

All that day Eugene labored to finish the task. *At breakfast,* his father had pointed that familiar gnarled finger at him and had given the word—no barn dance until the traps, all twenty-one of them, had been repaired. *Now the sun was low* and shadows were over all but the very tops of the firs. The sound of the dinner whistle *had long since died away.*

Without going so far as to begin every story with "Once upon a time," you should make sure that time is made clear and that changes in time are indicated. You should know the order of the events in your story and stick to this order. Time order in your story is just like time sequence in a paragraph.

The trouble that the girl has in telling about her experiences in the study hall (see page 90) is that she constantly has to go back to pick up things she has forgotten or dropped. She is a person trying to run with an armful of loose oranges. She should put all her oranges in a shopping bag by planning a time scheme and sticking to it.

Practice 33

A. The following paragraph has omitted all references to time. Rewrite the paragraph, inserting time words or phrases wherever a blank space is indicated. For example, you may wish to write the first sentence as follows: *"All through the long afternoon,* Greg worked on the motor."

_____ Greg worked on the motor. _____ he had completed the needed repairs. _____ he changed his clothes, pulled on his jacket, and _____ climbed into the cabin. _____ the roar of the engine satisfied him that all was in order, he taxied out to the end of the runway, where he sat _____, gunning the motor. _____, he eased the plane forward, faster and faster, until it lifted off the runway, _____.

B. Write a single paragraph in which you describe some common activity, such as the process by which you settle down to do your homework, or the steps you take in setting the table or doing the chores. Try to choose time words and phrases that not only give sequence to your actions, but that also give a sense of increasing importance or difficulty.

Stories exist in space. Go back for a moment to the Aesop fable of the Tortoise and the Eagle. Notice that there is no attempt to create any picture of the location. We do not see where the tortoise is; we don't know whether the rock that the eagle alights on is by the seashore or on a mountain. We have no way of knowing how the eagle takes hold of the tortoise, or of how the tortoise felt going up—or coming down. We don't know the kind of rock, other than that it is a "huge" one, on which the tortoise broke apart. In other words, Aesop makes no attempt to appeal to our senses. He does not make us see anything, smell anything, taste anything, hear anything, or feel anything.

A modern story, in contrast, is likely to be filled with writing that appeals to our senses. The scene of the action is pictured vividly, often with details that appeal to more than one of our senses. Most often, a writer uses visual pictures, since these are the most common. However, a good writer backs up his visual images with the other sense impressions.

Look again at the paragraph by Mary Austin, pages 93–94. Notice the sharp visual images—the "pool of waste full of weeds of a poisonous dark green," the three oaks "staggering" on the slope, the grass "thick and brittle and bleached straw-colored." So the most vivid language in the paragraph appeals to both sight and sound: the spring that "sobs and blubbers" in the "ashy-colored mud." The writer had heard the spring as well as seen it, and when she reports what she has seen and heard, the reader also sees and hears it.

There are two sides to the art of vivid writing. First, you need to observe, to see straight and clear, to listen, to feel, to become more aware of your surroundings. If you look at something carefully and see it exactly as it is, you should be able to shut your eyes and still see it.

Second, with the clear image of the object or scene in mind, you can *visualize* it as you write. Observing and visualizing are closely related. If you observe carefully in the beginning, you will visualize accurately later on.

Practice 34

Look carefully at an object or a scene for two or three minutes. For instance, you might choose to observe an object such as a pencil sharpener or a wall painting. Or you might study the view from the classroom window, being careful to limit the range of your observation to one small part of what you can see.

Then, shut your eyes for a moment and try to visualize what you have just observed, trying to picture as much detail as you can. Without looking again, write a paragraph in which you describe in interesting and clear detail what you observed.

Stories are about people. Actually, everything in a story is intended to tell something about people or about human nature. Even the tortoise's silly desire to fly tells us something about the impossible wishes and desires that people hold. People are the main part of a story. The plot and the background detail are useful chiefly because they let the reader imagine the human actions that are taking place. If your characters are not clearly drawn, you don't have a good story.

How do we draw characters clearly? Simply stated, we draw them the way they appear to us, just as we see the boy next door, the mailman, a teacher, or anyone. We draw him, first of all, *by what he looks like.*

Often, a simple description of his appearance will characterize a person well. If his hair is never combed, if he wears odd clothing, if he has habits or mannerisms or outstanding physical features, he becomes a special individual as soon as you point out these things.

Another way to describe a person is *by the way he acts* (*which includes how he talks*). It is easy to describe people with unusual or exaggerated ways of talking and acting. A bully, for instance, can be revealed in a very few words. We see him, hear him talk boastfully, and watch him push somebody around. It is harder to describe vividly more ordinary people, people who have little in their appearance or manner to set them off. In such cases, you must put all your powers of observing to work. You must study them, guess at what they are thinking, listen to their talk, and try to separate out those things about them which make them particular individuals.

Finally, you can describe a person *by what others say about him*. What another character in a story says about a person can often describe that person better than either an author's description of him or the person's own words and actions.

Furthermore, having seen someone through another's eyes, we often find ourselves, as readers, becoming interested in learning more. We make guesses about the character, find as we read that we are mistaken, and correct ourselves. We probably enjoy this kind of story more than one in which the author merely tells us that: "William Wertheimer was a good young man, kind to his crippled mother, a favorite with all the neighbors—a boy who delighted in leading old ladies across the street and walking miles to return lost articles to people. He was, in short, sober, dependable, worthy, hard-working—the kind of young man all of us dreamed of being."

Perhaps you can see how that information could be given a reader in a more imaginative, even more sporting, way, to let him make his own judgments. Suppose you had one of three toughs in black jackets lounging against the wall of a pool hall say, "Wertheimer? That cream puff? That goody-goody old maids' delight? He told me once he thinks work is fun and honesty is the best policy." A reader could not be sure, at that moment, whether to take Wertheimer seriously or to believe someone who by his general manner seems unreliable. Not quite knowing, a reader will go on to find out.

Practice 35

A. Think of a possible situation for a story, perhaps one that is wildly imaginative, such as a ship in distress at sea, a plane on a dangerous mission, or some other setting in which there is considerable action. Then, place a character in the midst of that story. How will you describe him: by your own words, by his own words and actions, or by someone else's words? Choose one method and draw the character as he might be in the setting you have created.

POINT OF VIEW

Even the simplest of stories must be told by someone, either by an outsider or person to whom the events of the story are happening. Aesop tells his story impersonally, speaking as a kind of reporter. Mary Austin writes as "I," speaking as herself. Other stories use more varied forms of these two methods.

Perhaps the easiest method is to be the all-knowing author. Here, the author knows all that is happening and can describe events just as he chooses. He is, in a sense, on both sides of a barn door at once; he can describe events on both sides at one and the same time. He can, if he chooses, dip inside the mind of any character and relate what the character is thinking.

A second method is for the author to tell the story as an observer who does not have the ability to know all. That is, he cannot probe the minds of the characters, but must report their actions and words to let the reader judge for himself. In a sense, the author is a camera; he goes into no minds, he reads no thoughts or feelings. He does not state, "Joe was hurt," but rather shows him jumping up and down, uttering cries of pain. He shows rather than explains.

A third method is to tell the story entirely from within the mind and senses, either of one of the characters, or of an observer who speaks as "I." Such a character cannot reveal what goes on inside the minds of others in the story, although he can reveal his own thoughts. If he is in the wrong position to see something—as, for instance, he may be on one side of the barn door pitching horseshoes while a fight is going on inside the barn —he cannot report what he cannot see. The author must take him inside the barn to see before he can report.

Practice 36

Write the beginning of a story, taking up no more than a page or a page and a half. Use one of the following situations as a start. You will have many elements to keep straight. You must introduce a character, perhaps more than one; you must set the scene; you must decide upon your point of view (will you tell it as "I" or will you be an all-knowing author?); you must establish an order of events in the proper time sequence; and you must be aware of having each event lead toward a possible climax—even though for this assignment you won't need to carry your story that far.

1. A boy—you or someone else—is sitting on the front lawn on a soft spring night waiting for his father to come home. When his father does get home, the boy will be punished for something he has done. During the time that you write of, nothing much actually happens—cars go by, a neighbor pauses to chat, maybe the moon rises. Your job is simply to make real and vivid a half-hour of the boy's waiting.

2. A girl—you or another—visits a friend's house the night before the class party and dance. She finds that the friend is not going to the party because her family could not buy her a new dress. Remember that here you will have to create a house, or at least a room in one, and two characters, one of them miserable. You will have to make up your mind how the situation might turn out, since the talk between the girls should lead toward some conclusion, even though you will not reach that conclusion.

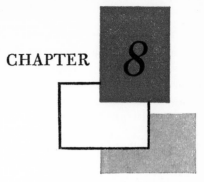

CHAPTER 8

Letter Writing

Probably the most frequent use for writing in everyday life is letter writing. A letter is the most useful means of written communication between people, whether they are very friendly or barely acquainted. Business firms in particular will tell you that writing letters is an important skill.

Most of us like to receive letters, and the surest way to receive them is to write them. The friend across country will enjoy hearing from you just as much as you enjoy hearing from him. Aunt Mabel upstate, who has been so generous, will look forward to your letter telling her how much you enjoyed her gift to you. Receiving mail is usually a happy occasion for all of us, young or old. In fact, for some, such as movie and television actors, politicians, and business firms, it is essential that they receive letters that comment upon their work.

THE FRIENDLY LETTER

First of all, let us look at some techniques to use when you are writing to friends, particularly close friends. Since your close friends are likely to be boys and girls your own age, with whom you have a number of common interests, your letter should contain the kind of news you would tell them if you were talking to them. What have you been doing? Have you made any trips, or taken part in any particularly interesting or unusual affairs? Do you have some new or exciting friends? Not only should your letter contain news about yourself, but it should also show your interest in things that are happening to or are interesting to your friend. Tell him how you have improved your batting eye since he last visited you and gave you some tips. If he has been ill, is he feeling better now? How was his trip back from the city? He is interested in you and what you have done, and will appreciate the interest you show in his affairs.

Every letter you write will have a purpose, even if it is just a letter to a good friend. You should also show your interest by writing as well as you can; no one appreciates a letter that is obviously hastily written, or written from a sense of duty without real thought or care. Here are some tips for writing letters:

1. Give information about your activities and show an interest in his.

2. Use easy, informal language, much as you would do if you were talking to him face-to-face. Just remember that he can't hear you say it, and be careful not to be too informal or abrupt in your writing.

3. Keep letters until you have answered them, so that you can refer to them when you reply.

4. As with all writing, think about what you are going to say before you actually start to write. For one thing, it will save you time, and for another, no one likes to receive letters that have many words crossed out or that are badly organized and difficult to read. You might even make a few notes about what you plan to say to be sure you won't forget anything and that there is some order to your writing.

As an example of good letter writing, look at this letter which Anne Frank wrote to her imaginary friend, Kitty.

Sunday, 27 September, 19___

Dear Kitty,

I just had a big bust-up with Mummy for the umpteenth time; we simply don't get on together these days. And Margot and I don't hit it off any too well either. As a rule we don't go in for such outbursts as this in our family. Still, it's by no means always pleasant for me. Margot's and Mummy's natures are completely strange to me. I can understand my friends better than my own mother—too bad!

Mrs. Van Dann had another tantrum. She is terribly moody. She keeps hiding more of her private belongings. Mummy ought to answer each Van Dann "disappearance" with a Frank "disappearance." How some people do adore bringing up other people's children in addition to their own. The Van Danns are that kind. Margot doesn't need it, she is such a goody-goody, perfection in itself; but, I seem to have enough mischief in me for the two of us put together.

If I take a small helping of some vegetable I detest and make up with potatoes, the Van Danns, and Mevrouw in particular, can't get over it, that any child should be so spoiled.

"Come along, Anne, have a few more vegetables," she says straight away.

"No, thank you, Mrs. Van Dann," I answer. "I have plenty of potatoes."

"Vegetables are good for you. Your mother says so, too. Have a few more," she says, pressing them on me until Daddy comes to my rescue.

Then we have from Mrs. Van Dann: "You ought to have been in our home; we were properly brought up. It's absurd that Anne's so frightfully spoiled. I wouldn't put up with it if Anne were my daughter."

These are always her first and last words: "If Anne were my daughter." Thank heavens I'm not!

Yours, Anne

Even though Anne knew no one would receive this letter, she wrote as if she were writing to a close friend.

You can learn much about writing letters to a friend if you study this sample. You can also learn much about Anne and the life she was leading at the time. A friendly letter should be like a mirror which reflects you and your activities to your friend. It should be vivid, intimate, informal.

Use stationery suitable for the letter you plan to write. It does not have to be fancy. The message is more important than the paper on which it is written. If you are writing a short message, use small-sized notepaper. If you are writing a longer letter, use stationery you have available. You may write on the back of each sheet if you need to.

Always use your best penmanship so that your friend can read what you write, and use ink. Friendly letters are not generally typewritten, although it is permissible to type them especially if you happen to be a good typist.

Practice 37

1. Write a letter to a close friend who is out of town on a vacation.
2. Write a letter to a favorite relative, telling him or her what you and your family have been doing.
3. Write a letter to a friend who has moved to another city recently. Include information about activities and mutual friends at the school you and he used to attend as well as information about yourself.
4. Write a letter to an imaginary friend to whom you can tell your innermost problems.
5. Write a letter to a friend who asked you to take his paper route or care for his pets while he is away, telling him how things are going.
6. Write a letter to a young cousin from whom you have just received an affectionate note written in a childish scrawl, his first attempt at letter writing. Remember that he is very young.
7. Write a letter to an older relative who is away at college.
8. Write a letter of congratulations to an older relative who is about to marry.
9. Write a letter to a friend who is ill.

10. Write a letter to a friend who has had an accident or misfortune.

THE SOCIAL NOTE

The thank-you note. The person who has invited you to visit, done you a favor, or sent you a gift, will appreciate a prompt note from you. Such a note need not be long, but it should be written as soon as possible. If you put yourself in the position of the person who extended you the favor, you will understand how much promptness is appreciated. A delay in your response could easily create an unfavorable impression: you didn't like the gift, or never received it; you didn't have a good time.

After you have expressed your thanks, briefly give some additional news about yourself or your family, your latest interests, plans, or activities. Just to say "thank you" might, in many circumstances, sound curt and ungrateful.

Write sincerely; say what you really mean. It is, of course, difficult to thank someone for a gift or a favor you didn't really care for, or to thank him for a visit you didn't really enjoy. However, if you give careful thought to the matter, you should be able to write a sincere message.

Here is an example of a letter written to express thanks for an invitation which cannot be accepted:

April 27, 19___

Dear Mrs. Melton,

You were so thoughtful to invite me to spend next weekend with you and Mr. Melton at your cottage on the lake. I still remember how much fun it was last year, and I would like nothing better than to go again.

But next weekend my father and mother are taking my grandfather up to Clinton, and I have to stay home to take care of the house. I just wish there were some way I could arrange to go to the lake instead, but I'm afraid I can't.

It was fun to see Audrey last Saturday. She and I enjoyed talking over old times again, particularly those we had at the lake last summer. It is good to see her looking so well again.

Again, many thanks; I wish I could be with you next weekend.

> Sincerely,
> Irene Davidson

Practice 38

Choose one of the following situations and write an appropriate letter.

1. A friend's parents have invited you to spend a week with them at their home in Florida.
2. A favorite uncle has sent you a string of beautiful pearls.
3. A friend has asked you to spend a week with him on a fishing trip. You don't like fishing, and you don't want to go.
4. An elderly aunt has sent you a gift that is far more suitable for a ten-year-old.
5. A friend has sent you the kind of gift you like to receive.

The bread-and-butter letter. A note written to a friend to express thanks for hospitality or some other favor or gift is often known as a "bread-and-butter" letter. Even if what you have received is something you don't want, remember that it was given in a spirit of kindness. It is difficult to express thanks for something you don't really appreciate, but you can always find something good to say, if only appreciation for the kindness of the giver. Remember that promptness and sincerity are absolute necessities in writing a "bread-and-butter" note.

Here is a typical example of a "bread-and-butter" letter:

> December 29, 19___

Dear Aunt Jean and Uncle Fred,

It certainly was fun to be with all the family this past Christmas, and I want to thank you for everything. Seeing you, Grandma and Grandpa Ferguson, and Roger and Timmy was like old times.

Many thanks, also, for the really fine necktie you gave me. I wore it with the new jacket that Mother gave me, when we all went to church last Sunday.

All in all, I was pretty lucky this Christmas. Spending the holiday with you was the high point, and I have my new jacket, tie, and a .22 rifle that Dad gave me.

Again, many thanks for everything.

> Sincerely,
> Charlie

It is quite likely that the writer of this letter was much more excited about the new rifle, but he is polite and sincere about what he says to his aunt and uncle. Even if he didn't like the tie, he was appreciative of the thought.

Practice 39

1. Write a thank-you note to an old friend of your father who took you and a friend to the theater.
2. Write a thank-you note to the parents of a close friend at whose home you stayed overnight. It was not a very interesting time, the food was only fair, and the sleeping arrangements were uncomfortable, but everyone was very friendly and treated you like a member of the family.
3. Write a thank-you note to a neighbor for putting you up for a night when an emergency in your family meant that you would be alone.
4. Write a note of appreciation to someone, a teacher perhaps, who performed a kindness for you in an unusual way.
5. Write a thank-you note to a friend of your brother who had been your host at a school party. You had a really wonderful time, and you would like to know him better.

The invitation. In writing a note to invite a friend or someone to a party or some other event, you should follow the same general suggestions for the friendly letter. However, you should be sure that your note contains information about the following points:

1. *what* the party or event is,
2. *when* it will take place,
3. *where* it will be held.

Add, too, such information as who is coming and what, if any, are the special things to do or bring.

Practice 40

Write two invitations for each of the following events, one to a friend and one to a relative.

a birthday party   a long automobile trip
a hunting or fishing trip   Thanksgiving dinner

THE BUSINESS LETTER

The business letter is more formal than the personal letter, and therefore the form you may use is much less flexible. If you observe the business letters that come to your house, you will see that there is a rather definite pattern, although business firms will sometimes alter the form slightly to suit their own purposes.

Writing a business letter is also an important skill to acquire, for there are many times when you may need to write one. You may need to send away for something, write a letter of application, or write someone or a firm for information or to lodge a complaint.

A business letter should be as brief and informative as possible. Look at the following example:

> 13 Arcadia Road
> Rochester, South Carolina
> August 7, 19___

Brighton's Hardware, Inc.
414 East Main Street
Rochester, South Carolina
Gentlemen:

I spoke to you yesterday concerning the mailbox I would like to order. At that time, I asked that my name plate be placed on the top of the box, but I neglected to ask that the street number be painted on the side of the box.

Would you please paint the number 13 on both sides.

> Very truly yours,
> Arthur P. Rowe

Notice that the writer of this business letter has followed a special procedure. He has put his own address and the date at the top of his letter, in the right-hand corner. Then, he has put the name and address of the firm to which he is writing over the salutation. The letter closes with the words "Very truly yours," a correct closing for a business letter. You may also say, "Yours truly," or "Truly yours," if you wish.

Practice 41

1. Write a letter to the Figmont Milk Company, requesting that they discontinue milk deliveries while you are on vacation.
2. Write a letter to the Rotary Club to thank them for their sponsorship of a community project in which you were involved.

The order. Many business letters are for ordering materials by mail. In many cases, an order form is supplied by the company, and you need only fill out the order blank carefully and completely to place your order.

If you order without using a blank, however, your letter must be very specific about the description of the item or items you want. If you have a catalog, be sure to list the item, its catalog number, the size you wish, the color, and how you intend to make payment, if a choice is offered. You may even want to list an optional item if what you want is not in stock. Finally, be sure to tell the company where to send the item.

Practice 42

Write a letter for one of the order problems that follow here. Think through what you are going to write before you begin.

1. Write to the Housewares Department of Sears and Co., 3804 Telegraph Avenue, Oakland 15, California, and order a set of dishes to be sent to your friend, Louise J. Martinez, Taxco, Mexico. Make up a catalog order number and other details.
2. Write to I. Magnin and Co., 2056 Broadway, Des Moines 8, Iowa, and order gloves for your mother. Give the size and color.

3. Write to the bike supply department, Montgomery Ward, 4622 East 14th Street, Roslyn, Long Island, and order a set of tires for your bicycle.
4. Write to Pets and Pals, Lafayette, Pennsylvania, and ask them to send you a list of the kinds of pups they have for sale. You may want to tell them what kind you yourself would like.
5. Write to Jim Duffy, manager of Kelly's Sporting Goods Store in Ashmont, Montana, and order equipment for a fishing expedition.

The letter of complaint or exchange. When you write a letter to request an adjustment such as a return of goods, a refund, or an exchange on an order, be sure to give exact details of the order and the reasons for your request. Perhaps you need a different size, or you don't like the color, or the merchandise you received was in poor condition. Tell why you are requesting the adjustment and what adjustment you think is fair under the circumstances. Refer to the invoice number or the date of the order in your letter. You can expect prompt action if you state your problem clearly and as briefly as possible. Remember, it is not necessary to thank the store in advance, and it is strategically unsound to threaten the company. The company is eager to have a satisfied customer. Just state your problem simply and clearly; let the company do the rest.

Practice 43

Select one of the problems or situations below and write a letter in which you request an adjustment. In each case, you decide what adjustment you wish to request.

1. A mirror purchased at Brier's at 22nd and Broadway in Byfield, Michigan, was delivered cracked.
2. The sweater you ordered at Kahn's, 13th and Broadway, Ukiah, California, is too large.
3. The hunting jacket you ordered from Sportsmen's Paradise in Altura, Pennsylvania, is too small.
4. The fruit you ordered from Bear Creek Orchards in Port-

land, Oregon, was so good that you want to order some to be sent to the friends you will name in your letter.

5. The bike you purchased through the mail order catalog of Montgomery Ward at 1385 East State Street, Salt Lake City, Utah, has faulty brakes.

The letter of application. A letter of application must also be specific. It must contain definite statements about you, such as age, education, and qualifications. It should offer as references people who have consented to vouch for you, your ability, and your work habits. It should contain a record of your previous employment. If you have any questions about the job, ask them courteously. In it you may request an interview at the convenience of the employer. In short, this letter is all about you. You must write a letter which presents you to your future employer in the best possible light, but you must be careful not to sound conceited or demanding. Though you will have to use the first person singular pronoun in such a letter, try to vary your sentences so that not every one begins with "I."

Here is a sample of a short but effective letter of application:

1525 B Street
Spokane 4, Washington
February 7, 19__

Personnel Director,
Spokane Recreation Department,
1328 Emerson Avenue
Spokane 3, Washington

Dear Sir:

I am applying for the position of playground director for the summer of 19__ and shall be available from the 15th of June to the 15th of September.

I have had both training and experience in this field. I am presently taking recreation courses at Whitman College in preparation for a major in physical education. Two evenings a week I assist the recreation director of the Crane

Neighborhood House. In the summer of 19___ I worked for the Recreation Department at Redwood Day Camp in the Montclair district. Mr. David Smalley, Director of the Crane Neighborhood House and Mr. Richard Owens, Director of the Injun Feather Camp, have the record of my employment and have agreed to furnish references for me.

At your convenience, I shall be happy to come to your office for an interview. After 4:00 P.M., I can be reached at 31 8-2171. Thank you for your consideration.

> Yours truly,
> John Hughes

Practice 44

Select one of the positions listed below and write a letter applying for it.

1. Boy salesman between the ages of 10 and 15 wanted for seed route in Fernwood, Indiana. Apply to Mr. B. Ingmire, Box X 356, General Delivery, Phoenix, Arizona.
2. Baby Sitters Attention! A baby sitters' Registry is now being established. Apply to Gloria Olson, 3786 South Towler Drive, Fresno, California.
3. Applications are now being accepted for positions of counselors' Assistants at the Redland Day Camp, which will be open from June 15 to September 15. Apply to Mr. Jay Van Gelder, Room 118, City Hall, 1025 Broadway, Manchester, Vermont. Boys and girls ages 12–15 are eligible.
4. Mother's helper wanted to assist with the care of invalid infant. Apply to Mrs. Herman Smith, R.F.D. 5, Walnut Creek, Ohio. Applicant must be dependable and strong, and between the ages of 12 and 15.

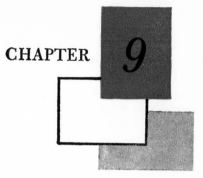

CHAPTER 9

The Oral Presentation

The most frequently used method of communication is speech. We must all talk in order to express our ideas, tell our needs, or explain our actions to someone else. As soon as we begin to speak, the listener begins to receive a message, not only from what the speaker is saying, but also from his way of speaking. Does the speaker's choice of words, enunciation, pronunciation, usage, and sentence structure indicate that he is a person of intelligence and education, or does he "put his foot into it" every time he opens his mouth? Our best chance of impressing a listener favorably is by speaking clearly and correctly.

CONVERSING WITH YOUR FRIENDS

All of you converse every day with the boys and girls in your classes. You don't usually have to plan these conversations, but you should think about making them as effective as possible.

Probably the first rule of good conversation is to listen. You have undoubtedly heard someone say, "I always enjoy talking to Mary (or Pete, or Sam). She is such a good listener."

You will become a better listener if you try to achieve a sincere interest and express that interest in what other people are saying.

Not only is it courteous, but also it may pay dividends in knowledge and understanding. Some points to remember are:

1. Listen with your mind as well as your ears. Pay the speaker the courtesy of listening to him, without letting your attention wander to someone else's conversation just beyond, or to what you expect to say when he has finished speaking.

2. React to his conversation. Ask questions that show your interest; show an appropriate reaction of surprise, concern, or sympathy. Don't be afraid to disagree, although you should be ready to back up your point. Disagreement should be expressed tactfully, and not just for the sake of disagreement.

3. Remember that a friendly smile and interest in the other speaker will go a long way toward beginning, maintaining, or renewing a friendship. If the other person is a new acquaintance, you have a particularly good chance to learn things about him that will help you to get to know him. He will very possibly give clues to his likes, interests, and hobbies.

4. As you tell your own experiences, include things that make your conversation lively and amusing. Speak simply and naturally, and do not dwell upon yourself. If you have something unpleasant to say or request, do it briefly and as courteously as possible.

Practice 45

Select one of the situations below. With a partner, act out a conversation to fit the situation. You may wish to demonstrate both the dos and don'ts for the situation.

1. You have just met your brother's roommate for the first time. However, your brother has told you much about him.
2. An elderly lady has come to call at your house. Your mother leaves you to converse with her as she brings in some tea. The elderly lady is not able to hear very well.
3. You have just been introduced to your blind date who turns out to be as shy and unsure as you are.
4. You have just met a very wealthy person who seems to belittle everything you do and all you have.
5. You have just met someone who has the same hobby you

have. From the first word you know you and he will be good friends.

6. You have just met Mr. Owens, who is hiring boys and girls to work at camp and is interviewing you.
7. You meet an old friend on the street several weeks after you had split up over a misunderstanding. You decide to say "hello."
8. At a get-together, you have met someone who knows you, but you cannot remember his name.
9. You ask a gas station attendant the way to Palm Springs.
10. You register a complaint with a store manager.

SPEAKING IN SCHOOL

There are, of course, many opportunities for more formal speaking in school. Recitations in class, oral book reports, research reports, student council reports, and even, perhaps, campaign speeches, all present challenges to us to speak clearly and effectively. The key to successful participation in these opportunities is in these three words: preparation, delivery, and evaluation.

Prepare for an oral report just as you would for a written report. Gather whatever facts you need for your presentation, and write them down, preferably in condensed form, for your report. Three by five cards are perhaps the most convenient means of keeping your notes in condensed form.

Delivery of your report is the critical point for your audience. If you have prepared carefully by having in mind what you want to say, as well as by having brief, well-organized notes you can refer to, you are well started. But the way in which you deliver your report will also have much bearing on the effectiveness of what you say.

Your English teacher or your speech teacher can help you increase your effectiveness as a speaker. However, there are some things you can do for yourself.

First of all, remember that, when you are speaking to the class, or to any audience, you are imparting information. Your speech is not just an ordeal to get through as quickly as possible. Therefore, do not hurry. If you hurry, you tend to slur your words and to speak indistinctly in many ways. There is probably no quicker way to lose an audience than to rush through a talk without giving the audience a chance to really understand what you are saying.

If you speak slowly, in a natural manner, making an effort to enunciate clearly, your report becomes that much more valuable, both for you and for your listeners. Speaking naturally also includes a natural variation of the tone and pitch of your voice. No one is inspired by a dull, dreary monotone.

A report given orally is only as good as you yourself make it. Therefore, it is up to you, with the help of your teacher, to evaluate the way in which you deliver your report. Evaluation can take place before, during, and after a speech. Most of us are a bit too nervous to make an evaluation during the giving of our report, but there are some things we can do. We can watch our audience to see if they appear to be grasping our thoughts. We may listen to ourselves as we go along, noticing if we are speaking in distinct tones, varying for emphasis, and enunciating properly.

Perhaps a more useful evaluation can be made before you deliver your report. Practice beforehand can give you many tips about what you are doing and about ways to make the actual report more effective.

As you talk, listen carefully. Taping your speech can often be useful. Do you speak in well-constructed sentences, avoiding long, involved constructions and difficult ways of phrasing ideas? Do you avoid using the same words over and over? Do you include interesting, although not necessarily long and difficult, words in your talk? Do you repeat yourself by using too often a favorite construction, phrase, or word? Do you use "uh" or "aahh" frequently? Does your tone of voice make you sound as if you are interested in what you are saying, or is it too loud or too soft, too monotonous or sing-song, or uninspiring in some other way? Do you enunciate clearly? Do you say "lidrachure" or "literature"? Is it "Ilikeyatuknow" instead of "I'd like you to know"?

Evaluation after you have given the report will consist mainly of finding out how effective your talk was. Naturally, your teacher can give you much help here. Find out in what ways your speech was or was not effective and then attempt to improve on your weak points.

Here are some exercises to help you, particularly in pronunciation and the use of your voice.

Practice 46

A. Now try some "tongue twisters." Repeat these sentences until you can say them clearly and smoothly. Remember: clarity is more important than speed.

1. Bertha bought better butter but it did not make the batter better.
2. Sarah sorted sea shells by the seashore.
3. The arrogant athlete asked Alfred about Althea.

B. Now try reading these sentences to a partner. Keep track of the endings you slur and give them more practice.

1. Ask your mother the width of her wrist.
2. The clown gasped when I grasped his flask.
3. The host asks most guests to mask.
4. A mist is a pest to birds in a nest.
5. The audience hissed when the villain, Mr. Grist, kissed the heroine.

C. Here are some pronunciation pitfalls to avoid. Repeat the correct pronunciations until you are sure you have them right.

1. Omitting sounds.
     govern ment—not "gummint"
2. Adding sounds.
     athlete—not "athuhlete"
3. Changing the location of sounds.
     in te gral—not "intregal"
     dis in te grate—not "disintregate"
4. Slurring words.
     What did you say?—not "wadjasay?"
     What is the matter with you?—not "wassamadawichoo?"

D. Speaking with expression is important. Practice saying the following sentences in several different ways, depending on the circumstances.

You opened the box.
The glass is broken.

1. As a question
2. As an expression of dismay
3. As an expression of disgust
4. As an expression of joy
5. As an expression of disinterest

E. As a further exercise in speaking, work out a dialogue around one of the following situations. Think of the way each sentence would be emphasized.

1. You and your hungry friend raid the icebox.
2. Your mother catches you tracking in mud.
3. You tell your father how you broke his favorite fishing pole.
4. You apologize to an irate neighbor for breaking her window.
5. You tell your sister how you lost her new sweater.

Vary the tone and pitch of your voice. Emphasize words you wish to stress. The meaning you see in the sentence will determine which words will receive relatively greater emphasis.

He did not do one homework assignment.

This sentence could simply mean that he did all the others, but failed to do one. If you think it means this, then you would read it like this:

He did not do *one* homework assignment.

The word *one* is emphasized, and the pitch of the voice remains about the same.

However, if you mean that the student did not do any homework, you would stress the first part of the sentence, and you would read it at a slightly higher pitch than you would the end of the sentence, stretching out the word *o-n-e*. Also, you would probably pause slightly after *one*. This is the way it would look:

> *He did not do o-n-e*
>
> homework assignment.

Changes in stress and pitch make your speech more interesting and colorful. These changes will help your audience share the emotion you feel as you speak.

Practice 47

Read the following passage aloud. Which words did you stress? Note how the pitch of your voice rises and falls.

The boy's knees felt weak. He tried to cry out, but his voice died in his throat. The great shark was circling slowly around the canoe. With each circle, it moved closer and closer. Now Mako could see the phosphorescent glow of the great shark's sides. As the fish moved in closer, he saw its yellow eyes and the gill slits in its throat.

Afa leaped from one side of the canoe to the other. In sudden anger Mako leaned forward to grab the dog and shake him soundly. Afa wriggled out of his grasp. Then, as Mako leaned to the left to catch him, the shift in weight tipped the canoe to that side, and the outrigger rose from the water. In another second, boy and dog would be overboard. Quickly Mako threw his weight to the right to balance the canoe, but with a loud splash Afa fell over into the dark water.

Mako stared after him in dismay. The little dog, instead of swimming back to the canoe, headed for the distant shore. And there was the great shark—very near.

"Afa! Come back!" Mako shouted. The dog turned back toward the canoe. He was swimming with all his strength. The boy leaned forward. Could Afa make it? Swiftly Mako seized his spear and stood upright. There was no weakness in him now. His dog was in danger of instant death.

Afa was swimming desperately to reach the canoe. The great shark had paused in its circling to gather speed for the attack. Mako raised his arm, took aim. In that instant the shark charged. Mako's arm flashed forward, all his strength behind the thrust.

The spear drove straight and true, right into the great shark's eye. Mad with pain and rage, Tupa whipped about, lashing the water in fury. The canoe rocked back and forth. Mako struggled to keep his balance as he drew the spear back by pulling on the long rope that connected the spear to his wrist.

He bent over to seize Afa and drag him aboard. Then he stood up, not a moment too soon. Once again the shark charged, this time at the canoe. Mako threw his spear, aiming for the other eye. The spear found its mark. Blinded and weak from loss of blood, Tupa rolled to the surface, turned slightly on his side. Was he dead? (From *Call It Courage*, by Armstrong Sperry. Copyright 1940 by The Macmillan Company. Reprinted by permission.)

CRITICAL LISTENING

We frequently hear sounds to which we no longer listen. Our minds have decided that many of the sounds around us are not important enough to listen to any longer. There are other sounds that are more significant for us. Our mental filter system, which discards many sounds as unimportant, such as the ticking of a clock, will alert us if it picks up a strange, new, unexplainable sound.

We also hear some sounds which do not require close attention. Background music is a good example. Research has shown that factory and office workers accomplish more when background music is being played. However, the workers do not consciously listen to this music. They are concentrating on whatever task they are performing.

We hear the motors of our cars, but do not listen to them unless some trouble develops. Then our mind starts to work on the problem to try to locate the difficulty. It is then that we must give close attention to the problem at hand. There are many other occasions requiring close attention, such as when instructions are being given or introductions are being made.

Our daily life, then, includes three levels of listening: unconscious hearing; hearing secondary to or incidental to another activity; and hearing plus listening. Here, we will discuss the third level, sometimes called *critical listening*.

Did you ever fail to get a passing grade because you didn't listen carefully when instructions were given? Did you ever have the embarrassing experience of introducing a new acquaintance whose name you hadn't listened to very carefully when you were introduced? All of us have had experiences which have taught us the need for paying very close attention at certain times.

In the classroom or at home, on the street, or on an airplane, our future and our very lives may depend on how well we listen. Whether the teacher is explaining something new, or a stewardess is telling how to use the oxygen mask, close attention is required.

Here are some suggestions for improving your listening habits:

Concentrate on what the speaker is saying. If it is important for you to be there to hear what he has to say, then devote your entire attention to his message. Don't "switch off" your mind and plan what you are going to do next weekend. Really concentrate.

Look at the speaker. It is a good idea to sit where you can see the speaker and where he can see you. You won't be so apt to wander mentally if you can watch the speaker.

Locate the main ideas. Information about *who, when, where, how, why,* or *what* is usually of prime importance in classroom instruction. It is a good idea to take notes when this information is being given. Many lecturers outline their speeches when they are preparing them and they stress the main ideas as they give them. Listen for these main ideas. When a speaker has finished, recall his main ideas.

Sit in a comfortable position. Slouching or slumping down until you sit on the back of your neck, or sitting with your legs awkwardly twisted under you will result in discomfort. An audi-

ence that squirms and twists is a distraction to the speaker. It
will be best for you and the speaker alike if you sit in a position
that will permit you to concentrate on the speaker rather than
on your aching joints.

Listen critically. Do you share the opinions expressed by the
speaker? Does the speaker support his statements by facts, or is
he making statements that have no foundation in fact? How
much of what he says is intended to appeal to your emotions,
instead of to your mind? In what ways do you disagree? Why?

Practice 48

1. Compare notes with a friend who heard the same talk, or
   the same instructions. You will be surprised how your reports will differ.
2. Give some rather detailed information to a friend. Have
   him tell you what he thinks you said. This can be even
   more surprising.

PART *II*

Grammar and Usage

CHAPTER *10*

The Function of Words

Words function in sentences in many different ways, that is, as these particular "parts of speech"; *nouns, pronouns, verbs, adjectives, adverbs, prepositions, conjunctions,* and *interjections.* A word may perform one function in one sentence and another function in another sentence. The classification of a word as a particular part of speech depends on the function the word is performing in the sentence.

> The *train* chugged down the track.
> The coach will *train* the team.

In the first sentence, *train* is the *name* of the line of railway cars on the track. In the second sentence, the word *train* tells what the coach will *do* to the team. Here is another example:

> I went to the *store.*
> The farmer will *store* the grain.

In the first sentence, the word *store* names the place where I went. In the second sentence *store* tells what action the farmer will take.

The **noun** is the part of speech that names.

The **verb** is the part of speech that expresses action or being.

Even if you do not know the meaning of a word, you can often tell whether it is a verb by the way it appears in the sentence. If you read, for example, "The man ataraxied down the street," you may wonder what he was doing, but you can guess that "ataraxied" is a verb by the way it is tied to the subject, "man." Another clue is that the word ends with "ed."

If you have trouble identifying verbs, test the word by trying to fit it into one of the following patterns, using the italicized verbs in the sentences at the left:

Let's *read* it.	He *did* _____ yesterday.
Let's *sing*.	He *will* _____ tomorrow.
Please *fix* it.	The dogs _____.
He *is* here right now.	Jim _____.
He *speaks* right now.	Let's_____it.
	Let's_____.
	Please_____it.
	Please_____.

Practice 49

A. Write the following sentences on a separate piece of paper. On a line to the right of each sentence, write *n* if the italicized word is a noun, *v* if it is a verb.

1. The *catch* on the door is broken.
2. We have a pretty little *dog*.
3. The *handle* of my purse is broken.
4. John will *drink* his cocoa.
5. The new car *handles* well.
6. Our *clock* is slow.
7. This cocoa makes a refreshing *drink*.
8. The policeman *dogged* the criminal.
9. The trainer *clocked* Pretty Boy.
10. Can you *catch* a fast ball?

B. Here are some words that can function as nouns or as verbs. Make a sentence for each and tell whether it is a noun or verb in each sentence.

1. sacrifice	4. study	7. step	10. control
2. fire	5. iron	8. bloom	
3. sense	6. package	9. scream	

THE NOUN

A **noun** names people, places, things, or ideas. The following words are nouns:

> people: friend, John, Betty, soldier
> places: Hong Kong, school, city, country
> things: train, pencil, boat, kite
> ideas: bravery, joy, hope, faith

You can also identify words that are nouns by testing whether they make sense when you use *the, an,* or *a* in front of them.

> *The* pupil is here.   *An* apple tastes good.
> *A* student won *the* prize.   *The* property was sold.
> *The* batter clobbered *the* ball.

Another test for a noun is that you can make it plural or possessive.

> Four pupil*s* went to the library to get their book*s.*
> Some apple*s* are now in season.
> The boy*'s* paper route has been increased.

Words like *the, a, an, some* or *three* are called *determiners* because they determine that the word that follows or goes with them is a noun.

You already use determiners appropriately to mark nouns in your speaking and writing. Here is a list of a few noun determiners used in the English language.

the	their	some	that
a	your	few	one
an	our	each	two
his	my	these	three
her		those	four
its		this	

Practice 50

A. Here is a list of nouns. Use each of them in a sentence that tells something about the noun. For example, you might use the noun "whale" in this sentence:

Whales are still hunted by men from sea-faring nations.

1. harpoon	6. kite
2. crab	7. fright
3. jaws	8. flying
4. macaroni	9. scene
5. adventure	10. pigeon

B. Each of the following sentences has two nonsense words in it. On a piece of paper write the nonsense word that you think is used as a noun. Then, to test your choice, rewrite the sentence substituting real words for the nonsense words.

1. Six wild *gorbles miggled* directly over our heads on their way north.
2. Several new boys had *thrabled* at the end of the *browbean* to await their assignments to class.
3. Placing the worn *regmeg* on the table beside him, the old man sat back and *laccupped* to me.
4. My mother *begorted* the oven door and took out a marvelously fragrant *snorl*.
5. Thinking he had *haskeled* his *mumfrow*, Abner went out to relax on the porch.

C. Select one of the sentences you wrote in the first practice in this set to be used as the lead sentence for a paragraph. In writing your paragraph, try to use nouns that are both precise and interesting. Remember also to make the sentences that come after the lead sentence develop the idea of that sentence.

Proper nouns. As you look at your list of nouns from the sentences above, notice that some are written with capital letters. Nouns that name *special* people, places, and things are called *proper* nouns and are written with capital letters.

Common Noun	Proper Noun
boy	Peter
girl	Susan

Proper nouns do not need determiners. You recognize them by their use in the sentence and by their capital letters.

Practice 51

Number from 1–10 on a piece of paper. Beside each number on your paper, write a C for a common noun, and a P for a proper noun. Then for each common noun write a proper noun, and for each proper noun write a common noun.

1. Budget Committee
2. Congress
3. book
4. woman
5. president
6. Bible
7. Betsy Ross
8. Lincoln
9. legislature
10. committee

Gerunds. Another kind of noun that is interesting is the *verbal noun,* or *gerund.* It is a verb form that functions like a noun, in that it names an activity.

> *Swimming* is fun.
> I enjoy *boating, rowing,* and *fishing.*

Note that these verbal nouns can pass the "determiner test." A determiner used with a gerund, however, is always a possessive word.

> *The* swimming is good along the coast.
> *His* rowing won the race.
> *John's* driving has greatly improved lately.

When an "ing" form functions as a verb, it "teams up" with a helping verb like *is* or *was.*

> He *was swimming* when the shark bit his leg.

Use the determiner test to help you decide whether one of these *ing* words is functioning as a noun or as a verb.

Practice 52

Locate the verbal *nouns* in the following sentences. Some sentences have more than one. Two sentences do not have any.

1. Studying is the key to success in school subjects.
2. Telephoning can be a great waste of time.
3. Understanding people is every teacher's job.
4. "Learning to use the Dewey Decimal System," said Eariel, "is your responsibility."
5. The boys went swimming at Lake Tahoe.
6. José watched the bullfighting in Barcelona.
7. The girls were practicing their scales on the piano.
8. Driving a truck is financially profitable.
9. Reading good books is one way to increase your store of knowledge.
10. "Throwing paper on the floor," said Miss Tank, "is not my idea of good conduct."

THE PRONOUN

A part of speech that is closely related to the noun is the **pronoun**. This word often takes the place of a noun, as its name indicates. (The prefix *pro* in pronoun means "in place of.") A test for a pronoun is to put a noun in its place.

The pronoun is very useful to the writer, because it can substitute for the noun and, in this way, lend variety to the composition.

Which of these two groups of sentences do you prefer?

> Bill fell downstairs. Bill broke Bill's leg.
> When Bill fell downstairs, he broke his leg.

There is no need to repeat the word Bill, because Bill certainly didn't break anybody else's leg when he fell! The pronoun "he" substitutes for the noun Bill and the pronoun "his" replaces the possessive noun "Bill's." Notice that the noun and the pronoun can be used in the same way in sentences. Here and on the next page is a chart of the most common pronouns:

I	you	he	she	it
mine	yours	his	hers	its
myself	yourself, yourselves	himself	herself	itself
me		him	her	

we	they			
ours	theirs			
ourselves	themselves			
us	them			
who	which	this	one	all
whoever	whichever	these	ones	some
whom	what	that	any	someone
whomever	whatever	those	anyone	somebody
whose			anybody	
whosoever			everyone	
whatsoever			everybody	

This list of pronouns is just about the same as it was in Shakespeare's day. Many nouns have been added to our language, but the pronoun list has not lengthened.

Practice 53

A. In the following selection, taken from a story about Amelia Earhart, locate the pronouns. You can see how their use adds variety and interest to the selection, if you substitute nouns in place of the pronouns.

> I do not know what became of the big shining Lockheed Electra, nor of Amelia Earhart, its pilot with the tousled hair, nor of Fred Noonan who wore a shamrock in his buttonhole for luck, and sat in the navigator's seat plotting the course by stars and sun. No one really knows what became of them; your guess is as good as mine. (From "Lost," from *A Bridle for Pegasus* by Katherine B. Shippen. Published by the Viking Press, Inc.)

B. Copy the following sentences on a separate piece of paper. Use suitable pronouns in the spaces provided. You may refer to the list on pages 130–131.

1. _____ named our new cat Gussie.
2. However, _____ found out that _____ was really a tomcat.
3. Then _____ had to rename _____ Gus.

4. Gus has whiskers four inches long. _____ are white and silky.

5. _____ cleans _____ every evening after supper.

6. Gus will purr for _____ who will feed _____.

7. The old lady cat, Frederika, does not like _____.

8. _____ is jealous of this gay young feline.

9. When _____ comes too close, _____ gives _____ a reminder to keep his distance.

10. _____ make a great pair.

C. Write a short narrative and use as many pronouns as you can. Exchange papers with a classmate when you finish. Make a list of the pronouns he has used. Did he find all the ones you used?

THE VERB

Earlier in this chapter you learned that **verbs** are words that tell what someone does or that something happened. The verb is the "spark plug" of the sentence. Every sentence must have one. The verb is also called the **predicate verb** of the sentence.

In the following selection, notice how the verbs give meaning to, or "spark" the rest of the words in the sentence. This selection is from the story of "Rip Van Winkle," by Washington Irving.

> "As Rip and his companion *approached* them, they suddenly *desisted* from their play, and *stared* at him with such fixed statue-like gaze, and such strange, uncouth lack-luster countenances, that his heart *turned* within him, and his knees *smote* together. His companion now *emptied* the contents of the keg into large flagons, and *made* signs to him to wait upon the company. He *obeyed* with fear and trembling; they *quaffed* the liquor in profound silence, and then *returned* to the game."

The verbs in the selection above told about something that was happening. A seventh grade student wrote the brief paragraph below. Note how vivid verbs give it life and vigor.

> "Fiddle-de-dee," exclaimed Jill as she raced over yards of paper with her crayons. As she turned, swooped, and

swirled, she made lovely big crayon marks on her paper. After doing this a few more times, she chortled, "Fiddle-de-dee!"—Michael Eastus.

Practice 54

A. On a separate piece of paper, number from 1–15. Opposite the correct numbers, write the verbs in these sentences from "Rip Van Winkle." The verbs all tell what someone or something did.

1. He rubbed his eyes.
2. The eagle wheeled aloft.
3. He recalled the occurrences before he fell asleep.
4. He looked around for his gun.
5. He found an old firelock lying by him.
6. Wolf had disappeared.
7. He whistled after him and shouted his name.
8. He grieved about his dog and his gun.
9. He dreaded to meet his wife.
10. He shook his head, shouldered the rusty firelock, and turned his steps homeward.
11. As he approached the village, he met a number of people.
12. With some difficulty, he found the way to his own house.
13. Rip's daughter took him home with her.
14. Rip now resumed his old walks and habits.
15. To everyone he met he would relate his experience.

B. Now write your own paragraph in which you show the value of lively verbs. Remember, though, the test is not how unusual your verbs are, but whether they express your meaning exactly. Use the dictionary to find synonyms for some of the verbs you ordinarily use.

Linking verbs. Verbs that link the subject with a word or group of words that follow the verb, but refer to the subject, are called **linking verbs.**

> Dr. Jones *is* a surgeon.
> He *has been* a member of the staff in a large hospital.

In these sentences, *is* and *has been* are linking verbs. Other linking verbs are *become, appear, seem, prove, remain, look, feel, smell, taste* and *sound.* Notice that they tell something about what the subject is or appears to be. The word or words following the verb mean the same as or describe the subject. These words are linked to the subject by the verb.

Practice 55

Join the following pairs of words in sentences of your own. Use the first word in each pair as the subject and join the second word to it by using a linking verb. Here is an example for you.

they _____ ready   They seemed ready for the examination.

1. night _____ black   6. you _____ ill
2. he _____ haggard   7. roast _____ edible
3. weather _____ cool   8. cat _____ happy
4. Albert _____ pitcher   9. sky _____ overcast
5. pie _____ good   10. man _____ astronaut

Tenses of Verbs. Verbs also have other traits without which we would have great trouble expressing our ideas clearly. Notice how the verbs in the following quotation from George Stewart's novel *Fire* enable him to shift quickly from one time to another.

> At this time of the wind-shift the fire had something of the shape of a long-barreled pistol, pointed downhill, with the grip turned in the down-canyon direction. The crew had run a line along the under side of the barrel and part-way around the grip. But now the south wind fanned up the flames, and from the upper side of the pistol-barrel the fire began to advance. . . .
>
> Slugger cursed violently to cover up his defeat. For a moment he hesitated, weighing the alternatives. . . . Early in the morning he would undoubtedly have chosen the bolder strategy. Now he chose the safer.
>
> "We'll flank her, boys! We'll catch her all right!" Then for the first time he tried to build up false courage. "This wind'll die down pretty soon!" And he added the rallying-cry of the hard-pressed commander: "They'll be gettin' reinforcements in to us pretty soon!" (From *Fire* by George

R. Stewart; copyright 1948 by George R. Stewart; reprinted
by permission of Random House, Inc.)

When Stewart describes the fire in the first two paragraphs, he
puts all the action in past time. But when he has Slugger speak
about what the fire-fighters are *going to do,* the author has to
shift to a future time.

Thus, a verb has different forms to show different times in
which something has happened, is happening, or will happen.
This makes it perhaps the most important part of the sentence; it
tells not only what action occurred, but when the action took
place. Without the verb, we would have little or no time sense.
Sometimes, of course, we use other words to show a change in
time. For example, we can say, "On Friday, I go to the city."
However, verbs are used much more often for this purpose.

The forms of the verb that indicate the various times are called
tenses. The term "tense" means "time." The forms of the verb
that indicate simple present, past, and future times are called
present tense, past tense, and *future tense.*

Present Tense	Past Tense	Future Tense
I talk.	I talked.	I shall talk.
He talks.	He talked.	He will talk.
They live here.	They lived here.	They will live in China.

Sometimes, though, these three simple tenses will not enable
us to express adequately the different times at which events
occur. For example, the author of the selection from *Fire* uses
the past tense to describe the action. Yet some actions in the
past happened before others that also happened in the past. The
writer must use a different tense to show the time of the action
that was completed first.

How do the different times in these three sentences affect the
meaning of each?

> He attends school in New York right now.
> He attended school in New York for five years.
> He has attended school in New York for five years, but
> now he is attending school in Roanoke.

Present perfect tense. This tense is formed by using *has* or *have* with the past participle of the main verb. (See pages 38 to 45 for the discussion of principal parts of verbs.) For example, "He *has attended* school for five years." This tense is used to show that something began in the past and is continuing on to the present time. It is said to be completed or "perfected" in the present time. Hence, we use the name "present perfect tense." You have used this and other tenses from the time you began to talk, although perhaps you have not been aware of it.

Here are some examples:

> They have played baseball for two hours.
> We have driven for two days.
> We have walked around town for an hour.

Practice 56

A. What effect does each of the verbs in parentheses have on the meaning of the sentence.

1. Slugger (cursed, has cursed) violently to cover up his defeat.
2. The crew (ran, has run) a line around the canyon.
3. The south wind (fanned, has fanned) up the flames.
4. Slugger (chose, has chosen) the bolder strategy.
5. The crew (fought, has fought) for several days.

B. It is important to be able to choose correctly between the past and present perfect tenses. Select a verb form for each of the following sentences. Be able to give a reason for your choice. Think of the sequence of time.

1. Last night the rain (fell, has fallen).
2. The barn door screeched as Fred (opened, has opened) it.
3. Ever since he was a young boy, Josh (wanted, has wanted) a pony.
4. On his trip into town yesterday, Josh's father (bought, has bought) him a pony.
5. During this summer, Josh (took, has taken) care of the pony.

6. At the end of the fight, Randy (threw, has thrown) Carl across the room.
7. For the past week, Randy (worked, has worked) every day at the ranch.
8. By the end of this chapter, the reader knows that he (read, has read) an exciting description.

Past perfect tense. Sometimes you wish to mention in one sentence two events which have occurred and have been completed in the past. If one incident happened before the other, you need to make this difference clear. Look at this sentence.

> After the fire had jumped the canyon, thick smoke began to drift overhead.

This sentence tells us that the fire had jumped the canyon before the smoke began to get close. The time sequence is clear. The first action was completed before the next one started. To show this time difference, we have to use the past perfect tense for the action that took place before the action described in the past tense. The past perfect tense is formed by using *had* with the past participle of the main verb. For example, "He *had attended* school for five years." Thus, the action that had begun in the past was also completed or "perfected" in the past.

Here are some other examples:

> Before he *moved* here, he *had completed* his schooling in the other town.
> They *learned* that he *had* already *received* his diploma.
> After the fire *had climbed* the bank, the smoke *eddied* again.

Practice 57

In the following sentences, one of the two verbs in parentheses expresses the time relationship accurately. Discuss why.

1. Before the rangers came, a scrap of glowing bark (fell, had fallen) on the catwalk.
2. The rangers reported that the fire (jumped, had jumped) another barrier.

3. This was the fourth summer that Slugger (fought, had fought) fires.
4. He hopes that he now (has, had) gotten into condition to play football.
5. Ben (flung, has flung) his fuses into the bushes after the fire (has, had) almost trapped him.

Future perfect tense. This tense is formed by using *shall have* (or *will have*) with the past participle of the main verb. You use this tense to express action beginning in the past, present, or future that will be completed or "perfected" before some later time. Here are some examples:

> By five o'clock, I shall have studied for three hours.
> By June, he will have been in this school nine months.
> By then, he will have arrived.

You will probably not use this tense as frequently as you do the others, but there might be instances in which you will need it.

These six tenses permit you to show almost any time of action or existence. The verb with its helping words, such as *have, has, had,* is the only part of speech that will allow you to indicate time merely by selecting a particular form.

Practice 58

A. In a selection you are reading identify the tenses of some of the verbs used. Perhaps you can find examples of all six tenses. After you have identified the times indicated by the tenses, try to explain why the author used the tenses as he did. If he occasionally used two different tenses in the same sentence, try to explain why he did so.

B. Write a paragraph or two about something in which you are presently interested. Tell how this interest started, if you can recall. Also tell what you are doing about it now and what you intend to do about it in the future. In writing these paragraphs, you will face the problem of indicating time clearly. Perhaps your teacher will ask you to read your paper aloud to the other students to see whether you have made your treatment of time clear in your account.

Perhaps you would rather tell how to do or make something, such as tying fishing flies or shaping the hull on a model boat. In such a paragraph, it is important that you show how each step follows the one before; time order must be correct.

Using the correct forms of verbs. Although a great many verbs probably never cause you any difficulty, a certain few may give trouble. Most of this section is devoted to the verbs that are often misused. If you have trouble with verbs, take this opportunity to learn how to use the correct forms. Fortunately, most English verbs do not give us trouble. The various forms of these verbs are made by simply adding "d" or "ed" or "ing" to the basic word. These verbs are called *regular verbs.* You may have trouble spelling the "ing" form on occasion, but the other forms are straightforward.

Most verbs have four basic or main parts. All other forms are derived from these forms. These four main or principal parts are named as follows:

Present	Present Participle	Past	Past Participle
help	helping	helped	(have, has, had) helped

In no form of a regular verb is the spelling of the basic stem changed. Here are the principal parts of some commonly used regular verbs:

Present	Present Participle	Past	Past Participle
talk	talking	talked	(have, has, had) talked
play	playing	played	(have, has, had) played
work	working	worked	(have, has, had) worked
state	stating	stated	(have, has, had) stated
jump	jumping	jumped	(have, has, had) jumped

Irregular verbs. As you already know, however, many of the commonly used and troublesome verbs do not form their principal parts in this regular pattern. Instead, they do so by chang-

ing the spelling of the original stem and even by becoming
different words. (A good example of these complications is the
verb probably most often used in English, *to be.*) These are
called *irregular verbs.*

Here are seven especially troublesome irregular verbs that are
widely used and often misused. Learn to use the verbs correctly
and readily by practicing aloud the correct forms in appropriate
sentences.

Present	Past	Present Participle	Past Participle (auxiliary plus the past participle)
(I) am (you) are (he) is	(I) was (you) were (he) was	being	(has, have) been
(I) come (he) comes	(I) came	coming (note spelling)	(has, have) come
(I) do (he) does	(I) did	doing	(has, have) done
(I) give (he) gives	(I) gave	giving	(has, have) given
(I) go (he) goes	(I) went	going	(has, have) gone
(I) run (he) runs	(I) ran	running	(has, have) run
(I) see (he) sees	(I) saw	seeing	(has, have) seen

Practice 59

In each of the following sentences, select the proper form of
the irregular verb.

1. Yesterday he (run, ran) for a touchdown.
2. You should have (saw, seen) how he eluded tacklers.
3. He had (went, gone) before the defense knew what had
   happened.

4. He (come, came) around the left end at full speed.
5. He has (gave, given) the team his best effort at all times.
6. They (was, were) surprised by his endurance.
7. He has (did, done) the most difficult tasks this season.
8. Have you (give, given) your speech yet?
9. Most of the boys (was, were) able to swim.
10. Norton (have, has) come with us.

More verbs. Here are troublesome irregular verbs. A common error made in using these verbs is that of substituting the simple past form for the past participle. Remember that the present perfect, past perfect, and future perfect tenses are formed by using auxiliaries such as *have, has, had, shall have,* or *will have* with the past participle: *have flown, have gone,* or *has frozen.* Notice that all the past participles of these verbs end in a somewhat similar sound of "en" or "n."

Here is a list of verbs given only in the troublesome tenses:

Present Tense	Past Tense	Present Perfect Tense
		(auxiliary plus past participle)
I blow	I blew	I have blown
I fly	I flew	I have flown
I grow	I grew	I have grown
I know	I knew	I have known
I throw	I threw	I have thrown
I break	I broke	I have broken
I choose	I chose	I have chosen
I freeze	I froze	I have frozen
I speak	I spoke	I have spoken
I steal	I stole	I have stolen
I swear	I swore	I have sworn
I tear	I tore	I have torn
I wear	I wore	I have worn
I eat	I ate	I have eaten
I fall	I fell	I have fallen
I take	I took	I have taken

Practice 60

Here are some examples of verbs given in the past tense and as past participles. On a separate sheet of paper write a sentence in which you use each form correctly. Remember that for each past participle you must supply an auxiliary.

1. spoke	6. chosen	11. broken
2. eaten	7. threw	12. stolen
3. took	8. ate	13. flew
4. knew	9. blew	14. frozen
5. flown	10. torn	15. wore

Other verbs. Here are more irregular verbs given in troublesome tenses:

Present Tense	Past Tense	Present Perfect Tense (auxiliary plus the past participle)
I begin	I began	I have begun
I drink	I drank	I have drunk
I ring	I rang	I have rung
I run	I ran	I have run
I shrink	I shrank	I have shrunk
I sing	I sang	I have sung
I sink	I sank	I have sunk
I spring	I sprang	I have sprung
I swim	I swam	I have swum

Practice 61

On a separate sheet of paper write the following sentences, using the proper form of the verb in parentheses in each sentence.

1. They (begin) their day yesterday with a dip in the icy lake.
2. They had not (swim) very long before their teeth started to chatter.
3. Some of them (sing) songs as they tried to be brave.

4. I thought some of them would have (sink) if they had stayed in the water longer.
5. When they eventually (spring) out of the water, they rushed indoors and (drink) hot coffee.
6. They (run) up the path with great speed that day.
7. Usually they wait until the breakfast bell has been (ring).
8. Today they waited before they (swim) in the lake.
9. My shirt (shrink) in the laundry.
10. Have you (begin) your homework yet?

More irregular verbs. Here are some more troublesome irregular verbs:

Present Tense	Past Tense	Present Perfect Tense (auxiliary plus the past participle)
I arise	I arose	I have arisen
I drive	I drove	I have driven
I ride	I rode	I have ridden
I rise	I rose	I have risen
I write	I wrote	I have written
I catch	I caught	I have caught
I feed	I fed	I have fed
I lose	I lost	I have lost
I make	I made	I have made
I shine	I shone	I have shone
I stand	I stood	I have stood
I teach	I taught	I have taught
I tell	I told	I have told

Practice 62

On a separate sheet of paper, write the correct tense of the verb in parentheses. Use the proper auxiliary for the present perfect and past perfect tenses. Number each sentence to match the numbers in the book. (Do not write in the book.)

1. This is the first year that I have _____ a car. (drive)
2. Previously I had _____ with him while he _____ me to drive. (ride, teach)

3. The finish on the car has _____ much brighter since we have been using this new wax. (shine)

4. I have _____ to the distributor to ask where we can buy the wax in this area. (write)

5. I had _____ Bud that I would let him know. (tell)

6. I had _____ because my parents had _____ me to stand when I am being introduced. (rise, teach)

7. Usually I have _____ by 7:00 a.m. (arise)

8. Yesterday morning I _____ my father to work. (drive)

9. What had you _____ your dog that morning. (feed)

10. Mrs. Simpson has _____ her wallet. (lose)

Verb look-alikes. Some pairs of irregular verbs resemble each other so much that many of us occasionally use one in place of the other, especially when we are speaking. Here are three such verb pairs: *lie-lay; sit-set; rise-raise.*

We use *lie, sit,* and *rise* when we wish to refer to some person's or something's being in or getting into some position:

Lie: to be in a horizontal position or to get into such a position; "to be or remain in a state of inactivity."

Here are some examples:

A patient *lies* in bed in the hospital.
The book still *lies* on the table in the living room.
His dog usually *lies* at the foot of the bed.

Sit: "to be seated"; "to rest on the lower part of the body."
Here are some examples:

He usually *sits* in this first seat.
Some cats *sit* on high furniture.
The microphone *sits* on a table in the front of the booth.

Rise: "to get up from a lying, sitting, or kneeling position."
Here are some examples:

We must all *rise* during the ceremony.
The sun *rises* over that mountain.
The audience *rises* when the President enters.

Here are the main forms of these irregular verbs:

Present Tense	Past Tense	Present Perfect Tense (auxiliary plus the past participle)
I lie	I lay	I have lain
I sit	I sat	I have sat
I rise	I rose	I have risen

The words commonly confused with *lie, sit,* and *rise* look much like them. However, their meanings are distinctly different. *Lay, set,* and *raise* are used to indicate that something is *being* put down or lifted up. In another sense, these words show the action of someone else on the object.

Lay: "to put or place (something) in a position of rest."

I'll *lay* the book on the table.
The doctor watched the attendants *lay* the patient on the bed.
That dog always *lays* a bone in the flowerbed.

Set: "to put in a particular place or position."

He frequently *sets* his lunch box on this bench.
The runner who *sets* a new record gets a special award.
Usually the milkman *sets* the bottles in the corner.

Raise: "to move (something) to a higher position; to lift up; to set upright."

The soldier *raises* the flag every morning.
Jack *raises* his marks each semester.
A witness *raises* his hand while he is being sworn in.

Here are the main forms of these verbs:

Present Tense	Past Tense	Present Perfect Tense (auxiliary plus the past participle)
I lay	I laid	I have laid
I set	I set	I have set
I raise	I raised	I have raised

Practice 63

On a separate sheet of paper write the proper tenses of the words in parentheses. Select the right word for each blank. Then, use the other word in a sentence of your own.

1. She always _____ the table before she _____ down to read. (set, sit)
2. Before the game starts, the spectators _____ while the flag is being _____. (raise, rise)
3. As he was _____ on the sofa, he _____ the book on the floor. (lay, lie)
4. Many people _____ to their feet when the exciting touchdown _____ hopes of winning. (raise, rise)
5. The outcome proved that they had not _____ in vain; so some fans _____ the captain to their shoulders and carried him from the field. (raise, rise)

THE ADJECTIVE

Words or groups of words that describe or limit the meaning of other words are called **modifiers.** One of the most important of these modifiers is the **adjective,** which is a word that describes or limits the meaning of a noun or pronoun.

> The *pretty* girl primped for the party.
> The *fat old* dog waddled into the house.
> The *French* teacher rolls her r's.
> The *three little* pigs fought the *big bad* wolf.
> He wrote the *scheming* villain a *scathing* letter.

Noun determiners, such as the articles *a, an,* and *the,* also function as adjectives modifying the nouns they indicate. The article-adjective *an* is used when the word that follows it begins with a vowel, and the article-adjective *a* is used before a word that begins with a consonant.

Practice 64

A. Now try adding adjectives of your own choice to these nouns. Note how the adjective improves or limits your mental picture of the person or object.

1. the _____ toad	11. _____ books
2. a _____ day	12. _____ window
3. an _____ beaver	13. _____ Mary
4. the _____ flower	14. the _____ trip
5. a _____ wall	15. _____ people
6. a _____ dog	16. _____ planets
7. the _____ cat	17. _____ moons
8. the _____ car	18. _____ sunshine
9. an _____ lake	19. _____ moonlight
10. an _____ show	20. _____ heart

B. Copy the following sentences on a separate piece of paper and underline the adjectives. Do not underline the articles *a, an,* and *the.*

1. The awkward hippopotamus can gallop with surprising speed.
2. The noisy, quarrelsome magpie is a cousin of the crow and has the same thievish habits.
3. Dad's favorite dessert is a pineapple cheesecake with a cracker crust.
4. All mammals have warm red blood and a four-chambered heart.
5. Utah has pink cliffs, white plains of sage, rugged black mountains, and colorful deserts.
6. The frightened little kitten fled.
7. The hard-hitting batter was walked.
8. Have the last autumn leaves fallen?
9. A bedraggled, brown puppy was whining.
10. Two speeding sports cars collided.
11. Timmy's huge red balloon burst.
12. A few muffled giggles could be heard.
13. The best safety poster has been framed.
14. Ichabod Crane was a tall, thin man with a small head, huge ears, large, green eyes, and a long, pointed nose.
15. When will the golden daffodils bloom again?

C. Read the following sentences aloud. Add adjectives that you think lend color and interest to the nouns.

1. We went down the _____, _____ road to visit _____ Uncle John.
2. I liked to go to my uncle's place because it was close to a _____ pool where we could swim and do _____ fishing.
3. The _____ door was open, so we went right in.
4. Uncle John seemed _____ to see us, and offered us _____ hotcakes and _____ bacon.
5. The _____ odors of the _____ food reached our nostrils as we approached the house.
6. After eating heartily, we settled down on the _____ veranda for a _____ chat.
7. Uncle John always has _____ tales to tell, some of them _____, some of them _____.
8. As soon as the day became too _____ for _____ talk, we changed into _____ trunks and sauntered through the _____ grass to the pool.
9. There we lay on the _____ bank and listened to the humming of the _____ katydids.
10. It felt _____ to doze and swim, and laze away the _____, _____ day.
11. Uncle John's place is the _____ idea of heaven on earth.

D. The following sentences come from "The Tallest Hat" by Ruth Adams Knight. Note how skillfully this author uses adjectives. A few, carefully chosen adjectives add life to a sentence the way a few, carefully chosen jewels make a plain dress more attractive. Too many adjectives "clutter up" a sentence, the way too many jewels clutter up a gown. Select the five adjectives from these sentences you find most striking and use them in sentences of your own.

The hat, a marvel of construction, was almost six feet tall. It had an intricate butterfly design that glowed with rich colors when the hat was illuminated by a little light fastened inside of it. * * * Shadowy figures moved in on either side of them. The streets became packed. Everyone stood in a velvet blackness that blotted out all but the outlines of the buildings against the starlit sky. * * * Hanni's ears now rang with a great clanging—a weird, rhythmic, almost barbaric beat. Then, above it all, she heard the imperative call of many horns. * * * These hats were from one to five feet in height, and their designs were beautiful to see. Lights within the hats made the richly colored paper glow like the stained glass windows of a cathedral. (From "The Tallest Hat," by Ruth Adams Knight. Reprinted by permission of Ruth Adams Knight and The *American Girl*, a magazine for all girls published by the Girl Scouts of the U. S. A.)

E. Sometimes adjectives are a hindrance rather than a help to good writing. Many adjectives such as *marvelous, grand,* and *terrific* are often overused and are nearly always vague or even meaningless. Too many adjectives where one or two are enough will also make your writing weak.

Rewrite the following passage leaving out or replacing the adjectives that are in italics. You may, if you wish, rearrange the order of words in some of the sentences. Then compare your rewritten version with some of the other versions in the class. How could your own version be made more successful?

What a *glorious* time we had at our annual picnic! The weather was *perfect;* only a few scattered *fleecy, white* clouds marred the otherwise *azure blue* sky of a *divine* and *beautiful* day. In the morning we played an *exciting, thrilling* and *hilarious* game of softball. We were all *exhausted* and *tired* when the game was over and we decided to plunge into the *clear* and *marvelous* water of the *inviting little* lake for a *cool* and *refreshing* dip. Then it was lunchtime. And the lunch was *superb*. We had some *scrumptious* hotdogs, *wonderful* salad, and a *delightful* cake baked by our *charming* and *gracious* hostess, Mrs. Russo. After lunch, we all went for a long and interesting hike in the *pretty* little wood that surrounds the campsite. When we left, we were a group of tired and dirty, but happy and grateful picnickers.

You learned previously that some forms of the pronoun show ownership. When these pronouns are used in order to modify nouns they are also called *possessive adjectives*. Look at these examples that follow:

> It is *my* coat.
> *Her* address is in the telephone book.

Here is a complete list of possessive adjectives:

Person	Singular	Plural
1	my	our
2	your	your
3	his, her, its, one's	their

Another kind of adjective is the *demonstrative adjective*. There are four such adjectives, *this, that, these,* and *those,* which are used to point out something. Here are examples using all of them.

> Put *this* book on *that* table.
> *These* coats belong to *those* people.

THE ADVERB

Adjectives, as you have seen, modify nouns or pronouns. There is another type of word that performs the function of limiting or describing. This word is called an **adverb**. Adverbs answer such questions as: Where? How? When? To what degree?

Adverbs may be used to modify verbs. Notice these sentences:

> There was *suddenly* a knock at the door.
> The knocking continued *loudly* and *persistently*.

The italicized words in these sentences each describe the way in which the verb expresses action or being. The first adverb, *suddenly,* answers the question "When?"; the second adverb, *loudly,* answers the question "How?".

In addition to modifying verbs, adverbs also modify adjectives and other adverbs.

Why did you leave *so* quickly?
In spring the foliage is *particularly* beautiful.

In the first sentence, the word *so*, an adverb, modifies *quickly*, another adverb. In the second sentence, the word *particularly* modifies *beautiful*, an adjective.

The correct use of adverbs can make your sentences both more accurate and more descriptive. Again, too many adverbs will clutter up your writing, just as will too many adjectives.

Practice 65

A. In the following sentences, pick out the adverbs and tell whether they modify verbs, adverbs, or adjectives. Notice that negative words, such as *not*, are used as adverbs.

1. Alfred seldom cares for dessert.
2. A really delicious sundae will not tempt him.
3. For Sunday dinner, he will take, instead, an extra helping of turkey.
4. Once I did see him eat a large, ripe banana.
5. He ate it with finely ground cheddar cheese.
6. Old Mrs. Bailey was severely frightened by the storm.
7. Soon we were able to pick out the figures on the shore.
8. Uncle Toby frequently visited our house.
9. Cats always keep themselves neat and tidy.
10. Rules are sometimes made to be broken.

B. Rewrite the following paragraph to make it more interesting. Add adjectives and adverbs, as well as more interesting verbs, to give it some life.

The man walked across the desert. He had walked a long time. He was thirsty and the sun was hot. He was lost and had no idea where he was going. After a while he began to see mirages in which water was waiting for him. He ran toward the mirage, and, when he found nothing, fell down from exhaustion. Finally, he got to his feet. As he did so, an airplane flew overhead. He waved at it, and it returned his signal. He was very happy.

C. Now, write a paragraph of your own. Describe a common happening in your home, such as your morning chores, getting ready for school, or other activity. Use adjectives, adverbs, and verbs carefully to give your story interest. Remember that overuse of descriptive words, or flowery language of any kind, is not good writing. When a verb itself is colorful or striking, it does not need adverbs; and when a noun is the *right* noun, it probably does not need adjectives.

COMPARISON OF ADJECTIVES AND ADVERBS

Often in writing and speaking, you will wish to compare the qualities of two or more persons or things. Adjectives and adverbs change their spelling to indicate the relationship between the items being compared. Note how the adjective *big* is used in these three sentences:

> The fox terrier is a bigger dog than the dachshund.
> The St. Bernard is the biggest dog in the world.
> I do not like a big dog.

In the first sentence, a comparison is made between two types of dogs: the fox terrier and the dachshund. In the second sentence, the writer is comparing the St. Bernard with all the other dogs in the world. In the last sentence, the writer is stating an opinion that involves no comparison. Note how the spelling of the word *big* changes in the first two sentences. These changes indicate degrees of comparison.

In the last sentence, there is no comparison, and the adjective remains unchanged. This form is called the *positive degree*. In the sentence that compares two types of dogs, the spelling of the word changes to the *comparative* form. When the comparison involves three or more persons or things, as in the second sentence, the *superlative* form is used.

> Positive (no comparison)—big
> Comparative (compare two only)—bigger
> Superlative (compare three or more)—biggest

Comparison can also be shown by using the word *more* with the adjective for the comparative form, and the word *most* with the adjective for the superlative form.

> He was *more* tired than Herbert.
> Maida was the *most* beautiful girl in the world.

The opposite kind of comparison showing a decreasing rather than an increasing amount is expressed by using the word *less* in place of *more,* and the word *least* in place of *most.*

> Robert was *less* discreet than Oliver in asking for money.
> He is the *least* able fireman in the company.

Comparison of adjectives. Follow these rules when you write the comparative and superlative forms of adjectives:

Adjectives of one syllable add *er* to form the comparative, and *est* to form the superlative.

Positive	Comparative	Superlative
short	shorter	shortest
tall	taller	tallest
large	larger	largest

Adjectives of two syllables form their comparative and superlative forms in two different ways:

1. Adjectives that end in *y* change the *y* to *i,* and add *er* for the comparative and *est* for the superlative.

Positive	Comparative	Superlative
lovely	lovelier	loveliest
happy	happier	happiest
heavy	heavier	heaviest

2. Other adjectives of two or more syllables use the word *more* for the comparative degree, and *most* for the superlative.

Positive	Comparative	Superlative
courteous	more courteous	most courteous
convenient	more convenient	most convenient

Some adjectives change their spelling entirely for the comparative and superlative forms.

Positive	Comparative	Superlative
good	better	best
bad	worse	worst
some	more	most
little	less	least
far	farther	farthest
many	more	most

Comparison of adverbs. Adverbs also have comparative and superlative forms. There are three ways in which adverbs are compared:

Use the word *more* (or *less*) with the adverb to form the comparative degree, and *most* (or *least*) with the adverb to form the superlative degree.

Positive	Comparative	Superlative
slowly	more slowly	most slowly
easily	more easily	most easily

Some adverbs use *er* and *est*.

Positive	Comparative	Superlative
fast	faster	fastest

Some adverbs change their spelling entirely.

Positive	Comparative	Superlative
well	better	best
much	more	most
badly	worse	worst

Practice 66

A. Write the correct degree of the adjective or adverb given before each of the pairs of sentences that follow:

1. *brave.* Dan is _____ than his cousin Ed. In fact, he is the _____ boy I have ever known.

2. *badly*. Paul sings _____. He is the _____ singer in the choir.
3. *well*. Charles swims very _____. He swims much _____ than his wife.
4. *friendly*. The _____ girl in the class is Maureen. She is always _____ to everyone.
5. *young*. Ed is young for his grade in school. He is the _____ boy in his class, but not _____ than some of the girls.

B. Number from 1–10 on a separate paper. Beside each number write the word that makes each sentence complete and correct.

1. Sandra is the (more, most) awkward girl in my class.
2. That show is the (less, least) exciting of all.
3. My broad jump was the (bestest, best) in the group.
4. They traveled (more far, farther) today than they did yesterday.
5. Stephen caught the (most, mostest) sand sharks.
6. Tony is the (least, less) studious boy in our homeroom.
7. Can Stella swim (gooder, better) than Marie?
8. Of the twins, Barbara is the (smarter, more smart).
9. She is the (more, most) contented person I have ever known.
10. Alice is (less, least) aggressive now than she was a year ago.

Problems in the use of adjectives and adverbs. Use adjectives, not adverbs, after the following linking verbs: *be, look, taste, smell, feel, sound, appear, seem, grow,* and *become.* (See pages 133 and 134.)

> This milk tastes sour (not sourly).
> The meat smells bad (not badly).
> I feel bad (not badly).

A good way to test the sentence is to substitute the word *is* for the verb you are using.

> The meat smells bad. The meat is bad.
> The milk tastes sour. The milk is sour.

Use adjectives to modify nouns and pronouns. Do not use adjectives like *good, real, sure, most,* and *near* as adverbs.

> (Correct) He voted for a sure thing.
> (Correct) He was surely tired.
> (Incorrect) He was sure tired.

Use adverbs to modify verbs, adjectives, or another adverb.

> (Correct) John was carefully trained.
> (Correct) Melanie swims well.
> (Correct) The jet travels considerably faster than a train.
> (Incorrect) Melanie swims good.
> (Incorrect) The jet travels considerable faster than a train.

Practice 67

Read these sentences aloud. As you read, select the word in parentheses that completes the sentence correctly.

1. He plays tennis very (good, well).
2. The flowers look (beautiful, beautifully).
3. My, how (bad, badly) the sewer smells!
4. My grandmother was (sure, surely) happy to visit us in the city.
5. Because of the terrible storm, the train (near, nearly) had a wreck.
6. When my brother arrived home late for dinner, my mother was (very, real) angry.
7. Bob could not write (good, well) after he had broken his finger.
8. Always write as (careful, carefully) as you can.
9. Danny felt (bad, badly) after his teacher had scolded him for what he did.
10. Ann plays baseball (real good, very well).

THE PREPOSITION

A **preposition** is a word used to relate a noun or pronoun to some other word or words in the sentence.

The boy *under* the house was hiding *from* his friends.
The ants *in* the cupboard attacked the cake.

In the first sentence, *under* shows the relationship between *boy* and *house*. The preposition *from* shows the relationship between *was hiding* and *friends*.

In the second sentence, *in* shows the relationship between *ants* and *cupboard*. Here is a list of common prepositions:

aboard	behind	from	throughout
about	below	in	to
above	beneath	into	toward
across	beside	like	under
after	between	of	underneath
against	beyond	off	until
along	by	on	up
among	down	over	upon
around	during	past	with
at	except	since	within
before	for	through	without

Sometimes, prepositions team up with another word to form a compound preposition.

because of	in spite of
down from	out of
on account of	

Compound prepositions function like a single word.

He came *down from* the ladder.

The noun or pronoun that follows a preposition is the *object* of the preposition. The cluster of words is called a *prepositional phrase* and the preposition is always the first word in the phrase. Notice the three italicized phrases in the following example.

He put the jar *on the table in the center of the room.*

Practice 68

A. Number your paper from 1 to 10. Finish the prepositional phrases in each of the following sentences.

1. The fish had the head of _____.
2. She hid the cookie jar on _____ of _____.
3. The creek ran through _____ and finally emptied out into _____.
4. The solution to _____ lies in finding the way to open the door to _____.
5. The boy stood alone on _____.
6. Skin divers have helped us to learn more about _____.
7. But divers cannot go beyond _____ in _____.
8. Silent shadows glided through _____ and eerie sounds came to _____.
9. The sergeant brought his platoon to _____ as the inspector stepped out of _____.
10. No light could be seen through _____ of _____ that stood on the shore.

B. Now write sentences each containing at least one phrase. Use these prepositions:

1. near	6. toward
2. until	7. above
3. between	8. against
4. before	9. up
5. behind	10. during

C. Locate the prepositional phrases in the following sentences. On a separate paper list the phrase and the word it tells more about. This word may be a noun or a verb. In the sentence, "The man *with the crippled leg* hobbled *down the winding road,*" *with the crippled leg* describes the man, and *down the winding road* tells where he hobbled.

1. The rows of swaying trees marked the boundary.
2. A barefoot boy with rosy cheeks trudged homeward.
3. A string of fish was drying in the sun.
4. Under a spruce tree slept the little, lost child.
5. "Wait for me," said Susan to Bob.
6. Where in the world did you get that piece of tar?
7. Pick a number from one to ten.

8. Put a pinch of salt into a cup of flour and mix it with a pan of water.
9. Thousands of lights shone from the windows of the building.
10. A pudding made of carrots and raisins tastes good at Christmas time.

PHRASES WITH NOUNS AND VERBS

You notice that prepositional phrases can relate to nouns, or they can relate to verbs. We know that words that relate to nouns are called *adjectives*. Words that relate to verbs are called *adverbs*. An adverb is a word or a phrase that tells *how, when* or *where* the verb action took place. Prepositional phrases, depending on how they are used in the sentence, may be either adjectives or adverbs. The prepositional phrase must always be as near as possible to the word it modifies.

Study these examples:

	Word	**Phrase**
When	now	in the summer
	then	at a later time
	sometime	between 12:00 noon
		and 1:00 p.m.
Where	here	in Sumatra
	there	under the house
	everywhere	in the cupboard
		amid the ruins
		from outer space
How	slowly	in a halting way
	quickly	with clumsy attempts
	sluggishly	
	sweetly	
	lovingly	
	sadly	
	carefully	

Practice 69

A. In the following sentences, you will find adjectives and adverbs, and adjectival and adverbial prepositional phrases. Copy the sentences on a separate piece of paper. Skip one line between each line of writing. Over each word or prepositional phrase that functions as an adjective, write *adj*. Over each word or prepositional phrase that functions as an adverb, write *adv*.

1. My cousin, Melissa, lives in Iowa.
2. The school in Bogota is attended by many Americans.
3. Because of a special arrangement with the United States, the American children with fathers in the consular service do not pay a fee.
4. Spanish is the language of the people.
5. A study of this language is interesting.
6. The student of Spanish learns that the rules for its use are many.
7. The rules for pronunciation are not very complicated.
8. The sounds of the language are like music to the ears.
9. Señoritas of Peru are as charming as they are beautiful.
10. I plan to make a trip to Peru in the spring to visit my cousin Melissa. Would you like very much to join me?

B. Select one of these sentences as the opening sentence for a paragraph about a personal experience. Use at least one prepositional phrase in every sentence. Remember, too, that good descriptive adjectives and adverbs, precise nouns, and vivid, lively verbs are necessary to make your writing come alive. When you have finished, go back over your paper to see if you can improve it in any way.

1. The school was new to me.
2. The main street was filled with holiday crowds.
3. I had decided to run away from home.

THE CONJUNCTION

The word **conjunction** means to join (*junction*) together or with (*con*). A conjunction is used to connect two sentence parts.

These parts may be words, phrases, or independent sentences.

Sal *and* Julius are good friends.
The cat ran into the room *and* under the bed.
The catcher threw quickly, *but* the runner was safe at second.

In the first sentence, the word *and* joins Sal and Julius, two words used in the same way as subjects. In the second sentence, *and* connects *into the room* and *under the bed*, both prepositional phrases which are equally important in describing where the cat went. They are thus used as adverbs modifying *ran*. In the third sentence, the conjunction *but* connects two clauses, *The catcher threw quickly* and *the runner was safe at second*. Both of these clauses could be used as single sentences, but here they are connected by the conjunction.

Words such as *and, but, or,* and *nor* are called **co-ordinate** conjunctions. Co-ordinate means, essentially, equal; thus sentence parts connected by a *co-ordinating* conjunction are equal parts, as in the examples above. Using conjunctions can often save words and make sentences much smoother. Look at the following two sentences:

Jane likes honey. Tom likes gingerbread.

Sometimes co-ordinate conjunctions are used to join two short sentences. The noun sentence is then called a *compound* sentence.

Jane likes honey, but Tom likes gingerbread.

Practice 70

Use conjunctions in order to join some of the sentences and to make this paragraph read smoothly.

The wind blew fiercely. The wind blew steadily. The small boat tried desperately to make the harbor. It wasn't making much progress. Soon, the waves began to rise higher. The waves began to splash over the bow. They began to splash into the cockpit of the boat. The lone sailor struggled to take down the sail. He could not do it. Then, a fierce gust of wind tore away the sail. It also broke the rudder. Soon, the wind swept the boat out to sea. The waves swept the boat out to sea.

THE INTERJECTION

An exclamatory word used in a sentence to express feeling or emphasis is called an interjection. *Ouch!* is a common interjection. Many, like *bah!*, are not really words. Others, like *wow!*, are listed in the dictionary as slang.

Often, an interjection has no relationship to other elements in the sentence.

> *Oh!* You startled me.
> *Alas!* The king is dead.

In other cases, it is used as part of the sentence.

> *Ah,* now I remember!

Here the emphasis is less strong.

Interjections are most frequently found in dialogue.

> "Oh, no!" she exclaimed in disbelief.

Always, they should be used with care. Their main purpose is emphasis, and overemphasis soon defeats its own purpose.

Practice 71

Write a sentence to go with each of the following interjections:

Help!   Whew!
Oops!   Ah!
Ouch!   Well!

CHAPTER *11*

The Principal Parts of the Sentence

A sentence has two basic elements: the predicate and the subject. Every sentence contains a visible predicate, and most sentences also contain a visible subject. In some sentences, however, the subject is not actually expressed; it is implied or understood. Even in sentences in which it is understood, the subject is, nevertheless, one of the most important elements.

THE SUBJECT

The subject of the sentence is the word or the group of words that identifies the "*do*er." It answers the question *who?* or *what?*

> Last summer *Bill* broke his leg. (*Who* broke his leg? *Bill*.)
> In the New England states the leaves turn red in the fall. (*What* turns red? The *leaves*.)

In other kinds of sentences the subject is the "receiver," the person or thing upon whom or which something is done.

> Bill was presented with a trophy. (*Who* received the trophy? *Bill*.)

In the New England states beautiful leaves are sold at the roadside stands in the fall. (*What* are sold? The *leaves*.)

In still other kinds of sentences the subject is the person or thing identified or described.

Bill is my brother. (*Who* is my brother? *Bill*.)
The leaves are very beautiful. (*What* are very beautiful? The *leaves*.)

A subject may be a word, a phrase, or a clause. The word may be a noun or a pronoun, and the phrases and clauses are often nouns.

Marianne visited the zoo today.
The little brown *dog* sat in the street.
The *wind* bent the willows.
Bob and *Mabel* worked on Sunday.
The *pen* and *pencil* fell to the floor.

In the above examples, words have been used as subjects.

Traveling by raft can be dangerous.
To make a long story short is sometimes difficult.

In the above examples, phrases have been used as subjects.

Whatever decision you make is all right with me.
Whoever wants to purchase a home may apply for a bank loan.

In the above examples, clauses have been used as subjects.

The **simple subject** is the noun or pronoun, without modifiers, that names the "*do*er," the "receiver," or the person or thing identified.

The long *row* of cars wound through the tunnel.
The red polka dot *dress* was sold.

The **complete subject** includes the modifiers of the simple subject. This is sometimes called a noun cluster, and the simple subject is called the headword.

> *The ancient tomb of the great Egyptian pharoah* was opened in 1952. (*The ancient tomb of the great Egyptian pharoah* is the complete subject; tomb is the simple subject.)

A subject may have two or more parts joined by the conjunction *and*. Such a subject is called a **compound subject**.

> *Jake and Don* built a dam.
> The *boys and girls* helped in the paper drive.
> The *pansies and the columbine* are blooming now.

A singular subject must have a singular verb at all times. A plural subject must have a plural verb. A compound subject requires a plural verb.

> Bill *is* waiting to see you.
> Bill and Jack *are* waiting to see you.
> The boys *are* waiting to see you.

Singular subjects that are joined by *or, nor, either . . . or, neither . . . nor* are singular, and require a singular predicate.

> Heidi or Alice is eligible.
> Neither rain nor snow stops the mailman.

Practice 72

A. Number your paper from 1 to 10. Write down the simple subject of each of the following sentences. The subject may have one part or more than one part.

> Jack ate the cake.
> Bob and Jack ate the cake.

1. The little white house stands near the beach.
2. John Silver gave me a note.
3. Betty and I found the place easily.
4. James Smith and Peter Crosby stood in the schoolyard.
5. A man who was wearing a gray hat rode through the gate.
6. The professor followed the turtle on hands and knees.
7. The turtle deposited her eggs in a sandy hollow.

8. The man and his wife listened attentively as their son played the violin.
9. A chill north wind whistled around the corner of the house.
10. The war-torn veteran and his bride settled in a peaceful valley.

B. Combine a subject group in column A with a verb in column B, adding modifiers to make complete sentences. Use each word in each column only once.

A	B
boys and girls	is
the dog	were
my friend	carries
Mabel and Louise	climb
Pete and Catherine	swim
I	talk
they	walks
Phil	has been
the kittens	like
the dragon	hears

C. Select the verb in the parentheses that is correct for the subject of each sentence. Remember that a singular subject requires a singular verb; a plural subject requires a plural verb.

1. The dog (is, are) an English setter.
2. The chattering of the monkeys (keeps, keep) me awake.
3. The remarks of the president (does, do) not prove anything.
4. Shoes for ladies (was, were) advertised at half price.
5. My father (is, are) an attorney.
6. The boys (was, were) throwing stones at the chickens.
7. Joan of Arc and Marie Curie (was, were) great women.
8. He (talks, talk) well.
9. My wife's uncle (was, were) elected chairman.
10. Ed and Mr. Sims (works, work) hard.

Usage problems.   Problems of usage arise in the agreement of certain subjects with their verbs.

Most indefinite pronouns used as subjects need singular verbs. The list of frequently used indefinite pronouns includes the following: *anybody, anyone, each, either, everybody, everyone, neither, nobody, no one, one, somebody, someone.*

> Someone has been eating the pie I set out to cool.
> Everyone is happy with the decision.
> Barbara and Francie were good students. Each of them was an outstanding athlete.

Certain common pronouns, *both, few, many,* and *several,* are plural and take plural verbs.

> Many are called; few are chosen.

A prepositional phrase which modifies a subject does not change the subject's number.

> A bowl of cherries was on the table (*bowl* is the subject).

Collective nouns like *group, family, public, number, band, committee,* and others usually require a singular verb, unless the noun is thought of as several *individuals.*

> The committee is ready to report.
> Our family was willing to participate in the experiment.

When the subject is a title, the name of a book, a clause, or a quotation, the verb is singular.

> *Gulliver's Travels* was written by Jonathan Swift.
> Whoever has the highest score is the winner.
> "Look to the highest" is our class motto.

Nouns endings in -*s* follow special rules of usage:

1. Nouns ending in -*ics* are singular when they refer to single branches of study, and plural when they refer to physical activities.

> Mathematics has always been her strong subject.
> Acrobatics are fun to watch.

2. Other difficult nouns ending in -*s* are the following:

> Usually singular: *news, measles.*
> Usually plural: *forceps, tidings, trousers.*
> Either singular or plural: *alms, headquarters.*

The forceps are on the table.
The news is good.

Sentences introduced by the word *there* present no problem if you remember two things:

1. *There* can never be the subject. It is an introductory word only.
2. The subject follows the verb which agrees with it in number.

> V   S
> There *were* ten *pennies* in the box.
> V   S
> There *is* no *question* about the right thing to do.

Practice 73

A. In the sentences on the following page, select the verb that agrees with the subject.

1. Each of the letters (was, were) rewritten.
2. There (was, were) good reasons for his absence.
3. The company (feels, feel) that your claim is valid.
4. Ten yards of material (was, were) required.
5. A tract of sixty acres (has, have) been purchased.
6. Neither of the books (belongs, belong) to me.
7. The United Cigarette Company (have, has) rented the building.
8. There (was, were) two windows in my room.
9. (Have, has) either of the two rooms been decorated?
10. *Tales of a Wayside Inn* (was, were) written by Longfellow.

B. Combine each subject in column A with a verb in column B, adding modifiers to complete the sentences.

	A		B
measles	gallows		is – are
few	everyone		was – were
each	group		has been – have been
number	several		talk – talks

THE PREDICATE

The **predicate** of a sentence is the part that tells what the subject did, or links the subject with words that relate to it.

> The rocket *went into orbit.*
> Jenny *is chairman of the committee.*

The **simple predicate** is the verb or the verb phrase (the main verb and its helpers) in the complete predicate.

> Sam *built* a boat.
> Mary *was injured* in the wreck.
> Josie *has been found.*
> Where *has* my dog *gone?*

Frequently used helping verbs include the following:

be (all forms)	shall	should	must
has	can	would	do
have	will	could	did
had	may	might	does

The **complete predicate** includes not only the verb or verb phrase, but also its direct or indirect object, the subject complement, and the modifiers of these parts. It is sometimes called the verb cluster, and the simple predicate is called the headword.

> Mary *wrote Jim a long letter full of interesting details.*

Here, the italicized part is the complete predicate or verb cluster. The word "wrote" is the simple predicate, or headword.

The predicate must be singular if the subject is singular. The predicate is plural if the subject is plural.

Dan *is* in room 39.

The boys *are* interested in sailing.

A **compound predicate** contains two or more verbs joined by a conjunction.

The teachers *sorted* and *recorded* the report cards.

The frightened puppy *jumped* through the fence, *ran* down the road, and *disappeared* from view.

The farmer *weeded* and *watered* his vegetable patch.

Practice 74

A. Copy the following sentences on a separate paper. Underline the whole predicate and circle the simple predicate. Remember that a verb may have more than one word.

1. A class was formed for a course in bowling.
2. Basketball and tennis are offered in the spring.
3. Some people have died from lung congestion.
4. We could hear the splashing of the children in the pool.
5. Everyone in the room was taking notes.
6. The lava flowed down the side of the hill.
7. Where have you been?
8. Has he been notified?
9. The secret of the cave will soon be discovered.
10. Open the door, please.

B. On a separate paper, underline the complete predicate in the following sentences. Circle the simple predicate.

1. He invited all the students in his class to his party.
2. Each girl wore a rose in her hair.
3. Whoever draws the lucky card will win the Pontiac.
4. The boys were shouting for help.
5. Ten reporters rushed for the telephone.
6. Students tardy to class must make up the time after school.
7. A trip around the world sounds exciting to me.
8. The girls made their own costumes for the plays.

9. Few students make the honor roll that many times.

10. When you are in an automobile, 100 miles is not very far.

THE ORDER OF WORDS

Let us now see how words can be adapted to the uses you want to make of them. Study the following sentences and observe how the word *point* changes in its meaning as its use changes. Which part of speech is it in each sentence?

> John *pointed* to his sister.
> His sister, Mary, was standing on the *point* of land.
> That was a *pointed* remark.
> Our team made fifty *points* in the last game.

Here are some variations on the use of the word *beat:*

> On the way home from school, Oscar *beat* up George.
> Mr. Harrison *beat* the rugs in the back yard.
> Gus is the policeman on the *beat.*
> Our team *beat* yours.
> Mother said after she did her shopping, "I am really *beat.*"

Practice 75

See how many different ways you can use the words *pool school, fall, run, air, bank,* and *trick.* Select three sentences for each.

Patterns of words and ideas. You have learned how words function as parts of speech in a sentence. Now see how the pattern of words changes to adjust to changes in ideas:

> The burn itched.
> The itch burned.

Suppose we substitute some words that don't make any sense and see if we can still get the idea.

> The ridlutz collobored.
> The collobor ridlutzed.

You can tell from the position of the words in the sentences that the person or thing that performs the act generally comes first, followed by the word that tells what he did. By changing the position of the words, you can change the function of the words and the meaning of the sentence.

One other clue made the meaning of these sentences clear, even when we used nonsense words. This clue was the pitch of your voice. You stressed the first part of the sentence and dropped your voice at the end of the sentence. The voice pitch pattern would look something like this:

> The collobor
> > ridlutzed.

Thus, the normal fixed order of a meaningful group of words and the change in pitch from high to low when we speak the final word make up the most frequently used type of English sentence. It makes a simple statement and is called a *declarative* sentence.

Fixed order in a statement. In studying the order of words in a declarative sentence or statement, let us call the first important word in the pattern S (the subject, or the word that tells *who* or *what* did something), and the next important word V (the verb or the word that tells what the subject did).

> S   V
> The boy winked.

Notice how the following subjects and verbs keep to the same pattern. Even those that make little sense, such as "flower sang," have a kind of pattern.

S	V
boy	scratched
girl	winked
bird	wilted
cat	bit
dog	kicked
tree	ran

S	V
flower	sang
fish	called
football	grew
friend	died
it	rolled
he	dug
you	screamed
they	cavorted
we	waggled

Remember that the symbol S refers to the subject (the person, place, or thing that performs the act); and V refers to the verb, or predicate verb (the word that tells what the subject did).

Practice 76

Pick out the subjects and the predicate verbs in each of these sentences. Underline the subjects once and the predicates twice. Write "S" over the subject words and "V" over the predicate verbs.

1. The old policeman's pony had stumbled and fallen.
2. On a clear, still night the lights from both sides of the channel glitter like stars against a velvet sky.
3. We all clapped, and some of the fellows whistled.
4. "Nagaina was coiled up on the matting by Teddy's chair, within easy striking distance of Teddy's bare leg, and she was swaying to and fro, singing a song of triumph."
5. Out on the prairie a coyote yelped and the dogs of the camp barked.
6. On a ridge Walter climbed a tree.
7. Twenty feet below him the froth-covered sea rumbled and hissed.
8. Now, miraculously, the skies cleared.
9. The wind moved into the southeast.
10. The temperature dropped to 23°.

Fixed order in a question. In a question, the fixed order is somewhat different. Sentences that ask questions are called *inter-*

rogative sentences. Study these questions. Can you work out the pattern of S and V? Note that the predicate has more than one word. (If you have trouble working out the pattern, turn each question into a statement first.)

> Have you studied?
> You have studied.

1. Do you swim?
2. Will your father come?
3. Can he refuse?
4. Would you walk?
5. When shall we go?

It is apparent that the fixed order in a question is $V - S - V$. If the predicate has only one word, the pattern will be $V - S$. Notice that when you speak a question the pitch of your voice rises at the end. The voice pitch pattern would look like this.

> he?
>
> Does

Fixed order in a command. Remember that a simple sentence can *make a statement, ask a question,* or *give a command.*

Examine the sentence, "Smile, please." Where is the subject? The subject of a command is understood, or assumed. The sentence is really, "(You) smile, please." Note that the predicate is expressed; so the pattern of fixed order in a command sentence is $(S) - V$.

Let us now review our three patterns.

> Statement—(Bill smiled) $S - V$.
> Question—(Did Bill smile?) $V - S - V$.
> Command—(Smile, please.) $(S) - V$.

Reminder: There may be more than one subject or more than one predicate in a simple sentence. (See page 85.) Note also that the predicate must be plural if the subject is plural.

> *John* and *Jack* run.
> $(S + S) - V$

Pronouns in sentence patterns. Look back at the pronoun chart (pages 130–131). Now use *I, he, she, we, they,* and *who* in sentences of your own. Now use *me, him, her, us, them,* and *whom* in another set of sentences. Notice that *I* does not "fit" in a sentence where you used *me,* and *him* does not "fit" in a sentence where you used *he.* Can you tell why?

Practice 77

Now study these sentences. What pronouns function as subjects.

1. I saw Bill today.
2. He made a speech in class.
3. Do you know Bill's girl friend? She lives right here in our town.
4. My girl and I saw her with Bill yesterday at Fifth and Main.
5. They were crossing the street.
6. We called them several times, but they apparently did not hear us.
7. Who knows?
8. Maybe they will marry.
9. He and Jane were chosen to play the leads.
10. She is Miss America.

You will recall that the subject normally appears in the first part of the sentence pattern in a simple statement. In the sentences above, *I, he, she, we, you, they,* and *who* appear in the subject position in the pattern. The pronouns *me, him, her, them, us,* and *whom* are direct objects and never appear in the subject position, unless you want to talk like a TV Indian: "Me go"; "Him bad Injun." On pages 181–182 you will read more about the uses of pronouns as direct objects.

Practice 78

A. Number your paper from 1 to 10. Write the S and V words of each of the following sentences to show the fixed-order patterns.

1. The sharp, explosive crackle startled him.
2. He arrived at the forks at half past twelve.
3. George worked on his project with much care.
4. The man and his dog were last seen in Scarsdale.
5. Peter Abramowitz, in his best suit and new shirt, applied for the job at the supermarket.
6. The brief day drew to a close in a long, slow twilight.
7. What have you done with my pencil case?
8. Close all the windows before leaving, please.
9. You and I will write and direct the spring play this year.
10. You should not have come with us without permission from the principal's office.

B. In this exercise, write sentences to fit the patterns given. Notice that where a double pattern is given, (S + S) or (V + V), a compound subject or verb is called for.

1. (S) V
2. S V
3. (S + S) V
4. S (V + V)
5. (S + S) (V + V)
6. V S
7. V S V
8. V (S + S) V
9. (S) V
10. S V

C. Now make up ten sentences of your own. Show the pattern of fixed order in each.

Reminders:

1. Check each to be sure you started with a capital and ended with a suitable end punctuation.
2. Check each to be sure it gives the reader a sense of completeness.
3. Read each aloud to be sure your voice pitch at the end of each word group indicates a true sentence.
4. Be sure each sentence expresses only one idea.

D. Now write sentences according to the instructions given.

1. Write five sentences that have a single subject and a single verb. SV
2. Write five sentences with more than one subject and a single verb. (S + S) V
3. Write five sentences with a single subject and more than one verb. S (V + V)
4. Write five sentences with more than one subject and more than one verb. (S + S) (V + V)
5. Write five questions. VS? *or* VSV?
6. Write five commands. (S) V

Summary. A sentence is a group of words containing a verb and also a subject (either expressed or understood), and ending with a change in the pitch of the voice (or a mark to indicate such a change) to signify the completion of what the speaker started to say.

The subject is the word (or words) that is tied to the predicate and tells whomever or whatever the sentence is about.

The predicate verb (predicate) is the word (or words) that tell something about the subject and give the reader the feeling of completeness.

A sentence may have any one of a number of word patterns, and the sentence is complete when the pattern is complete.

Practice 79

Pick out the complete subjects and predicates in these sentences adapted from *Walden,* by Henry Thoreau.

1. In the fall the loon came to Walden Pond.
2. The woods ring with his wild laughter.
3. At rumor of his arrival all the sportsmen are on the alert.
4. They come rustling through the woods, at least ten men to one loon.
5. But now the kind October wind rises, rustling the leaves and rippling the surface of the water.
6. The waves rise and dash angrily.

7. They seem to take sides with all waterfowl.
8. Then our sportsmen must beat a retreat to town and un-finished jobs.
9. I frequently saw one of the stately birds sailing out of my cove.
10. And so I left him disappearing far away.

THE DIRECT OBJECT

You learned that the subject and predicate verb are in a certain order in a simple sentence, and that the subject is the noun (or nouns) that tells who or what did something. Look at the sentence, "Clara baked a cherry pie." Who baked a cherry pie? The answer is, *Clara.*

You also learned that the predicate verb is the word or words that tell what the subject did, or said, or was, or thought. In the sentence, "Clara baked a cherry pie," the word *baked* tells what Clara did. In the sentence, "The ball broke a window," the word *broke* tells what the ball did.

You will have seen, also, that the verb generally comes after the subject in a simple sentence and has the second position in the pattern.

Now suppose you should meet someone who said, "Clara baked. . . ." You would wonder what Clara baked. Your conversation might go like this:

> Joe: "Clara baked."
> John: "Clara baked what?"
> Joe: "Clara baked a cherry pie."

You can see that the words "a cherry pie" complete the idea of the verb. In these sentences, what noun or group of words completes the idea of the verb?

> The Dodgers played a fine game of baseball.
> They made three runs in the ninth inning.
> One of their opponents committed an error.

Then the pitcher threw a wild pitch past the catcher.
Finally, the Dodger's slugger hit a home run.

We call the word that completes the meaning of the verb the **object** of the verb.

Now, look at these sentences and see *where* the object comes in the sentence.

The California Indians ate acorns.
They ate bugs, too.
They roasted the bugs.
Sometimes they ate rabbits.
They used shells for money.
We have found piles of these shells.
They moved their homes frequently.

The direct object of the verb is the *third* part of our pattern. We can mark the direct object O.

Practice 80

Now go back to the sentences above and mark each word that fits into the pattern S – V – O. Here is a sample of what you are to do.

S   V   O
The California *Indians ate acorns.*

Finding S–V–O in a question. The sentences you have studied so far have been simple statements of fact. Now let's look at a question, and see what kind of pattern can be worked out.

Has your car a horn?

To help work out the pattern, turn it around to say:

Your car has a horn.

The pattern is clear.

S   V   O
Your car has a horn.

Put the sentence back into its original form.

V   S   O

Has your car a horn?

From this exercise you can see what the pattern of a question is.

V   S   O

If you have a question that has a verb with two parts, the pattern may be:

V S V   O

Did John wash the car?

Practice 81

A. Number your paper from 1 to 10, skipping a line between each number. Write the S, V, and O words for each sentence in the order they are now in. Then, rewrite the sentence to make a sentence with the order of S–V–O.

1. Has Sam driven the car?
2. Will Joe make a homer?
3. Do you like chocolate cake?
4. Will Mary frost the cake?
5. Did the milkman leave the butter?
6. Will you get some eggs?
7. Does Joan like her job?
8. Were the girls washing the car?
9. Is Mr. Kirk visiting them this week?
10. Will you open the door?

When you have a question that starts with *where, when, why, who,* or *what,* the pattern will be a little different. In these questions, it will help to turn the question into a statement in order to see the pattern more easily.

B. Write 10 statements of your own. Mark the S–V–O where you think it comes in your sentences.

C. Write 10 questions of your own and mark them for the S–V–O pattern. Then, rewrite the questions so that the order becomes that of a statement. Can all questions be rewritten in this way without adding or subtracting words.

Finding S–V–O in a command. You are quite experienced in finding S–V–O now, and this last pattern should not be hard to do.

Look at this sentence:

Shut the door!

You will notice that a sentence that gives a command does not have a subject expressed; it is understood. The person who gives the command is really saying, "(You) shut the door!" The pattern for this kind of a sentence situation is:

(S)   V   O

Practice 82

Now find the S–V–O in these sentences (a few may not have O).

1. Study your lesson.
2. Do the dishes.
3. Pick up the papers.
4. Eat your spinach.
5. Turn off the TV.
6. Shut the door.
7. Iron the handkerchiefs.
8. Call the dog.
9. Turn on the lights.
10. Burn the rubbish.

Pronouns as direct objects. Back on page 175 as you studied pronouns you used them as subjects. However, pronouns also function as direct objects. When they do, some of them change their form.

Changes of form to indicate the different uses of a word have just about disappeared from our language. The forms given below are the last remnants. Those used for the subject are called

nominative, or subject forms. The forms used for the direct object
are the objective, or object forms. The objective forms are also
used for pronouns that are objects of prepositions.

	Nominative (subject)		**Objective** (object)
Singular	I	*Singular*	me
	you		you
	he		him
	she		her
	it		it
Plural	we	*Plural*	us
	you		you
	they		them
	who		whom

Note the difference in use:

> *We* will visit Europe soon.
> Dick will take *us* to the plane.
> Susan will wave good-by to *him*.

Practice 83

Now make a list of the pronouns in the following sentences
and tell whether they are nominative (subject) or objective
(object) forms.

1. Do you see her and him?
2. They are coming toward us.
3. You can see them if you try.
4. Shall we go to the show with them?
5. I enjoy being with her.
6. He is a good sort and so is she.
7. What did you do with it?
8. Who is your best friend?
9. Ask him to bring the girl whom I met yesterday.
10. She is the one with whom he is walking now.

THE SUBJECT COMPLEMENT

You have now become familiar with the simplest sentence patterns in English: subject–verb and subject–verb–object. In the following paragraph look for a new sentence pattern in the italicized sentences.

> The meat hung in the smokehouse. Jody ran to it and swung open the heavy timbered door. *The smokehouse was dark and cool. It was odorous with the smell of hams and bacons. It was dusty with the ash of hickory. The rafters were bare.* Three shoulders of ham hung, lean and withered, and two bacon sides. Old Slewfoot had indeed done damage. *The meat was dry but tender.* Jody touched his tongue on it. *Its saltiness was not unpleasing.* . . . (Reprinted with the permission of Charles Scribner's Sons and William Heinemann, Ltd. from *The Yearling* by Marjorie Kinnan Rawlings. Copyright 1938, Marjorie Kinnan Rawlings.)

In these sentences, a new element, the subject complement, has been added. A complement is a word that completes the verb and *renames* or *describes* the subject. Words that rename, either nouns or pronouns, are called *predicate nouns* (or *pronouns*). Words that describe are called *predicate adjectives*. The sentence pattern is S–V–SC, or subject–verb–subject complement.

Practice 84

Select the subject, verb, and subject complement in the italicized passages in the paragraph above and write them under the appropriate headings.

Subject	*Verb*	*Subject Complement*
Smokehouse	was	dark (and) cool

Verbs such as "seem," feel," and "look" *link* nouns, pronouns, or adjectives to the subject. Note the following sentences:

> The children *seem* tired.
> The parents *feel* sad.
> The boy *looks* happy.

In these sentences, the verbs express little or no action, but only a condition or state. They are *linking* verbs which join the subject complements to the subjects. Here is a list of common linking verbs, including the forms of the verb "be."

is	has been	look
was	had been	become
am	may have been	seem
are		sound
will be		

The pronoun used as a subject complement deserves special attention because it is often misused. Notice the subject complement in each of the following sentences:

> The speaker was *he*.
> The teacher is *she*.
> The caller was *I*.
> The winners are *they*.
> The losers are *we*.

In the sentences above, the changed positions of the subject and subject complements would result in the following sentences:

> He was the speaker.
> She is the teacher.
> I was the caller.
> They are the winners.
> We are the losers.

Thus, you use the subject form rather than the object form. You know you have used the correct pronoun if it functions just as well when the sentence is reversed.

You will have noticed that adjectives may also complete the meaning of a sentence with a linking verb by describing the subject.

Observe these sentences:

> The girl is *tired*.
> The bus is *late*.
> Our team is *happy* over the victory.

The italicized words are adjectives describing the subject. They answer the questions: What kind? How many? Which one?

Practice 85

A. Copy the following sentences, adding a subject complement in each.

1. The tree is _____.
2. It will be _____ in the spring.
3. Its blossoms are _____.
4. Mr. Jones is an _____.
5. He is very _____.
6. His work is _____.
7. The books are _____.
8. The girl seems _____.
9. The answer sounds _____.
10. He became _____.

B. The symbol for a linking verb is LV. The symbol for a subject complement is SC. Now write some sentences of your own using the patterns given below. Some of these patterns require a direct object and some require a subject complement. Remember that the subject complement may be a noun, pronoun, or adjective.

1. S LV SC
2. (S + S) LV SC
3. (S + S) LV SC
4. S LV (SC + SC)
5. S + S V O
6. S V O
7. LV S SC?
8. (S) V
9. (S) LV SC
10. S (V + V) O

C. Write a paragraph of several sentences to tell how you felt the first day you came to a new school, or about some other big event in your life. Does your paragraph contain more direct objects or more subject complements? Why?

THE INDIRECT OBJECT

You have learned how nouns and pronouns are used as subjects, direct objects, and subject complements. Now you will study another use for these two parts of speech—the indirect object.

> Mary gave Jim a book.
> Sam wrote John a letter.
> I sent him some cookies.

In these sentences you will recognize S–V–O and will observe that something new has been added. This new element in the sentence is the **indirect object**. It names the person *to* or *for* *whom* something was done or said. As in the examples above, the preposition *to* or *for* is often understood. Note that the verb expresses an action. We do not have direct and indirect objects after linking verbs—verbs that express a state of being.

Here are some other examples:

> We sent our *friends* gifts.
> Later they wrote *us* letters.
> I will show *you* some of them.

In these sentences, the word in italics is the indirect object.

Practice 86

A. Number your paper from 1 to 10. Rewrite the following sentences adding an indirect object where blanks appear in the sentences.

1. The waiter handed _____ a check.
2. They gave _____ free tickets.
3. Please give _____ your paper.
4. Draw _____ a camel.
5. You can mail _____ a box of cookies.
6. Send _____ a box, too.
7. Many people give _____ money.
8. The students sold _____ tickets.
9. The captain handed _____ a mop.
10. Linda sent _____ a postcard.

B. Copy the following sentences. Place an S over the subject, a V over the verb or predicate, O over the direct object, and IO over the indirect object. What do you observe about the sequence DO and IO?

1. John sent Bill a postcard.
2. Bill gave him a receipt.
3. They bought us sodas.
4. We gave the waiter our order.
5. The fountain boy served us the order quickly.
6. Gerry promised us a picnic.
7. The storm brought the farmers some much-needed rain.
8. The cold weather gave him the sniffles.
9. Our teacher assigned us some homework.
10. Mother allowed me fifty cents for lunch.

C. Here is another opportunity to write sentences from patterns. When we add the indirect object, the pattern will look like this: S V IO O. Write sentences using these patterns:

1. S V
2. S (V + V)
3. (S) V O
4. (S + S) V IO O
5. V (S + S) V IO O?
6. (S) V IO O
7. (S + S) (V + V) O
8. S (V + V) IO O
9. S V (IO + IO) O
10. S V (O + O)

Remember: nouns and pronouns serve as subject, direct objects, indirect objects, and subject complements. These words are also referred to as "completers" of verbs.

Remember also:

> Subject–verb–Ind. Object–Direct Object
> Subject–linking verb–Subject Complement

Practice 87

A. Write ten sentences that contain direct objects and indirect objects, or subject complements. Mark the complements with DO, IO, or SC.

B. Copy the following sentences, marking the subject, predicate, direct object, indirect object, and subject complement. (Not all five will occur in every sentence.)

1. The wind carried his hat over the lake.
2. These garments are second-hand clothes.
3. The parish includes all of southern Coalinga.
4. Since we wish to limit our list, we have not included medical journals.
5. The owner gave the campers three rules: that they cut down no trees, put out all fires, and clean up all rubbish before leaving.
6. A reckless driver endangers the lives of all people around him.
7. During the ceremony the bridegroom gave his bride a ring.
8. South of Craney Island is Portsmouth.
9. Ask Dr. Blosser what he will do.
10. His services were invaluable.

C. Write sentences to fit these patterns:

1. S LV SC
2. S V O
3. V S V IO O
4. LV S SC
5. (S) V O

CHAPTER 12

Phrases and Clauses

PHRASES

A phrase is a group of related words that functions as a single part of speech. A phrase does not have a subject or predicate.

Phrases offer writers ways to add variety to their sentences. They add important details which create interest and supply additional information, and they make it possible to begin sentences in different ways. Within a sentence, phrases provide short cuts to avoid longer and more awkward constructions.

Note how the italicized groups of words in the following examples form a unit. These units are called phrases.

> *In the morning* Bob takes the dog *for a walk.*
> When the weather is warm, my friends all like *to swim.*
> The canary chirped happily *in his cage.*
> *Paddling vigorously,* John reached the other side.
> *In the refrigerator* is a poor place to keep bananas.

Phrases are of three kinds: verb phrases, prepositional phrases, and verbal phrases. You studied verb phrases (see page 169). Here you will study prepositional phrases (see pages 156 to 157) and verbal phrases.

The prepositional phrase. A prepositional phrase consists of a preposition, its object (a noun or pronoun), and any modifiers of the object. (Refer to page 56 for a list of prepositions.)

> When Jim cycled *to school,* he carried his books *in the basket on the handlebars.*

The italicized words are prepositional phrases.

to (prep.)   *school* (object of preposition)
in (prep.)   *basket* (object of preposition) *the* (modifier)
on (prep.)   *handlebars* (object of preposition) *the* (modifier)

Practice 88

A. On a separate piece of paper, write the prepositional phrases in the following sentences.

1. We scrambled for those seats that were still left in the football stadium.
2. We saw a salamander under a rock.
3. The boy with the checked shirt is my brother.
4. Last night we observed a ring around the moon.
5. Sally walked against the wind on her way home from school.
6. Beyond the blue horizon lies a city of gold.
7. The rough tongue of the puppy raised goose pimples on my arm.
8. Stories about the Northland gods explain thunder and lightning.
9. Every man on a submarine is carefully trained.
10. Under the bed is the place where dust gathers easily.

B. Make up ten sentences that include the following prepositional phrases. Underline the phrases.

1. above our heads   6. after a short visit
2. at noon   7. within a short time
3. by that time   8. beside the brook
4. on the roof   9. for some time
5. between the rows   10. to the moon

A prepositional phrase may function as an adverb. An adverb phrase modifies a verb, an adjective, or another adverb.

> I saw a lark *in the tree.*

The prepositional phrase *in the tree* tells where I saw the lark. It is functioning, therefore, as an adverb.

> *On September 8,* he met Tom *in West Virginia.*

In this example there are two prepositional phrases that function as adverbs.

> *On September 8* tells "when."
> *In West Virginia* tells "where."

Practice 89

Copy the following sentences on a separate piece of paper. Underline the prepositional phrases. Indicate the word that each phrase modifies.

1. One day last week Elizabeth watched television until midnight.
2. The actors in the play performed with skill.
3. The class made a protest over the interruption.
4. The windstorm died down in the late afternoon.
5. Sue had to return home for an interview.
6. The highway will run through a tunnel.
7. The two boys met behind the barn to plan their afternoon's adventure.
8. King, our dog, ran into the water to get the ball.
9. Up in the attic you will find an old umbrella.
10. The teacher dropped her book on the floor.

A prepositional phrase may function as an adjective. An adjective phrase modifies a noun or pronoun.

> The girl *in the green dress* is related to Eloise.

The phrase *in the green dress* modifies *girl* and functions as an adjective.

Dan bought a car *with a fancy horn.*

An automobile *with automatic transmission* is generally more expensive to operate.

Bertha purchased a house *among the trees.*

The phrase *with a fancy horn* modifies *car* and therefore is used as an adjective. *With automatic transmission* and *among the trees* are both used as adjectives since they modify nouns, *car* and *house,* respectively.

Practice 90

Add prepositional phrases to each of the following sentences to expand them into longer and more interesting sentences. In parentheses after each sentence, tell whether the phrase is being used as an adverb or an adjective.

1. The teacher knew a short way home.
2. One day Joe met a boy.
3. The odor was unpleasant.
4. The pansies are blooming vigorously.
5. A foreign car passes our house daily.
6. Please bring me that coat.
7. The Cub Scouts enjoyed watching the game.
8. Please list names in the middle column.
9. I saw our mascot.
10. Nathan's teacher sent him a book.
11. Peter brought home a basket.
12. Have you read this collection of stories?
13. Mrs. Wrenn bought three cakes of soap.
14. Steve questioned his German teacher.
15. The bottle of dye is sitting there.
16. Her dog stole a pound of butter.
17. We have several arithmetic problems to do.
18. The private smartly saluted the lieutenant.
19. Prices are going higher every day.
20. A stately procession wound its way slowly past.

Note that on a few occasions a prepositional phrase may be used as a noun, especially in spoken sentences.

> *Over the fence* is out.
> *Inside the tent* is cozy and warm.

The verbal phrase. A verbal phrase consists of a verbal (a participle, a gerund, or an infinitive), its object, and any modifiers. A verbal is a word that originates from a verb. Here are examples of a participial, a gerund, and an infinitive phrase in sentences:

> (participle) The boy *playing ball* is a good first baseman.
> (verbal noun or gerund) *Playing ball* is his favorite sport.
> (infinitive) He likes *to play ball*.

A **participial phrase** consists of a participle and its related words. The participle may end in -*ing* (present participle), or it may end in *ed, t*, or *n* (past participle). You studied participles earlier on pages 134–139, learning that a participle is the second or fourth principal part of the verb.

A participial phrase functions as an adjective. In the sentence given in the first example above, the phrase *playing ball* modifies *boy*.

Here are other examples of participles and their uses.

> Throwing off his coat, the foreman grabbed a shovel. (*throwing* is the participle and *throwing off his coat* is the participial phrase modifying the subject, *foreman*)

> He gave his canteen to the soldier lying beside him. (*lying* is the participle and *lying beside him* is the participial phrase modifying the object of a preposition, *soldier*)

Practice 91

A. Find the participial phrases in the following sentences. Copy the sentences on a separate piece of paper. Underline the phrase and indicate the word it modifies.

1. The brown bear wounded by the bullet limped into the woods.
2. Jane saw Jack walking up the street with Laura.
3. Beverly pulled from the fire a letter burned beyond recognition.

4. Marion rescued the lost sheep caught in the berry patch.
5. Tired from his long walk, Don sat on the porch.
6. Tempted by a three-layer chocolate cake, Eloise broke her diet.
7. Calling her family around her, the quail started down the path.
8. Unnerved by the horrible sight, the little boy sat down and cried.
9. The little puppy, still chasing his tail, bumped into the door.
10. The church seen through the mist offered sanctuary.

B. Use each of the following participles in a sentence.

1. called	6. stolen	11. climbing
2. probing	7. landing	12. crumpled
3. worried	8. smiling	13. annoyed
4. introduced	9. swimming	14. loved
5. eaten	10. laughing	15. running

Sometimes the punctuation of a participial phrase presents problems. Here are some rules to guide you.

1. Use a comma after a participial phrase at the beginning of a sentence, if the phrase can be dropped without altering the meaning of the sentence, set it off with a comma. If it cannot be dropped use no comma.

> *Tugging on his halter,* the stallion indicated his wish for freedom.

2. Use a comma to separate from the rest of the sentence a participial phrase that is not necessary to the meaning.

> John Glenn, *encased in the capsule,* circled the globe.

Practice 92

Copy the following sentences on a separate piece of paper. Insert commas where they are needed.

1. Opening the door of the school Cuthbert entered wagging his tail.

2. There he met the principal looking stern and severe who banished him into the street.
3. The street filled with boisterous children is no place for a dog, Cuthbert decided.
4. Back he went into the school filled with friendly faces.
5. "That dog must go" stormed the principal completely unnerved by Cuthbert's audacity.
6. "Phone the S.P.C.A.," he stormed. Encouraged by the principal a secretary called the S.P.C.A. to come for Cuthbert now completely cowed by his cold reception.
7. In a few minutes a kindly old man used to the ways of a dog came for the now penitent Cuthbert.
8. As Cuthbert departed his tail wagging gently and somewhat morosely seemed to be saying "It's a dog's life, after all."

The gerund phrase. A **gerund phrase** consists of a gerund, its object, and modifiers.

A gerund is the second principal part of the verb and, therefore, can be recognized by its *ing* ending.

The gerund phrase always functions as a noun. In the following sentence the gerund phrase *playing ball* is the subject of the sentence.

Playing ball is his favorite sport.

In this sentence, the gerund phrase is serving as the direct object of the sentence.

Tom likes *playing ball.*

In this sentence, the gerund phrase is used as the subject complement.

His hobby is *playing ball.*

Notice that a gerund may be a single word or part of a gerund phrase.

Swimming is good exercise.
Swimming the English Channel is a dangerous undertaking.

Be careful to distinguish between a gerund and a participle that ends in *ing*. Remember that the gerund is always a noun and the participle is an adjective. Neither one uses an auxiliary verb when it is part of a verbal phrase.

Practice 93

A. Copy the following sentences on a separate piece of paper. Underline the gerund phrases. Tell whether each is used as the subject, direct object, or subject complement.

1. Locating the criminal will take some time.
2. Speeding on the highway is not as serious a crime as speeding in a residential area.
3. The elderly lady enjoyed sitting in the sun.
4. When Sue was asked her favorite pastime, she said, "I enjoy swimming in the rain."
5. Studying for a test is not very much fun.
6. One of life's satisfactions is doing your best.
7. Excessive speeding on the highway is a crime.
8. Migrating to America would give many foreigners pleasure.
9. Jumping rope and playing jacks are favorite amusements.
10. I watched boxing in the gymnasium.

B. Write ten sentences using gerund phrases as subjects, direct objects, or subject complements. Underline the gerund phrase and label each to indicate its function.

The Infinitive Phrase. The **infinitive phrase** consists of an infinite, its object, and modifiers.

An infinitive is the first principal part of the verb and has the word *to* before it. Thus, the infinite form of the verb *run* is *to run;* the infinitive forms of *carry, burst,* and *eat* are *to carry, to burst,* and *to eat.*

An infinitive phrase may function as a noun, adjective, or adverb. In this first sentence the infinitive phrase functions as a noun and is used as the subject.

>   *To tell the truth* is not always easy.

Here the infinitive phrase functions as a noun and is used as the direct object.

> Richard wants *to tell the truth.*

Here the infinitive phrase functions as a noun and is used as a subject complement.

> The best plan is *to tell the truth.*

Here the infinitive phrase functions as an adjective modifying *failure.*

> The convict's failure *to tell the truth* led to his conviction.

Here the infinitive phrase functions as an adverb, modifying *wait.*

> The doctor did not wait *to tell the truth.*

Sometimes the word *to* creates confusion, since it is, as you will remember (see page 157) also a preposition. Remember that *to* followed by a verb is an infinitive while *to* followed by a noun, perhaps with intervening modifiers, is a preposition.

> He tried to climb to the top of the mountain.

Here, *to climb* is an infinitive and *to the top* is a prepositional phrase.

Occasionally, the infinitive phrase appears without the word *to;* it is, nevertheless, an infinitive.

> The king called for everyone to eat, drink, and be merry.

There are three infinitives in this example: *to eat, (to) drink,* and *(to) be.*

Practice 94

A. Locate the infinitive phrases in the following sentences. Tell what part of speech each is according to function.

1. I decided to attend the show.
2. Mabel was anxious to phone the company.
3. To summarize was impossible in the short time allowed.

4. "To be another Barrymore is my ambition," sighed the would-be actor.
5. He went to get his bike.
6. The war to end all wars was a failure.
7. The fat lady wanted to occupy the whole bench in the park.
8. He phoned to tell me that he was going to Detroit.
9. To locate the missing heir required the services of ten detectives.
10. The people settled down to wait for the basketball game to begin.

B. Write ten sentences in which you use an infinitive phrase as the subject, direct object, or subject complement.

C. Write ten sentences in which you use the infinitive phrase as a noun, adjective, or adverb. Underline the phrase, and label the part of speech it is.

Misplaced modifying phrases. Confusion often results in a sentence when a modifier is set in the wrong place, or lacks a word to modify. Modifiers, either words or phrases, should be placed close to the word they modify so that the meaning will be absolutely clear. Here are examples of correctly and incorrectly placed modifiers:

> (incorrect) I saw the Empire State Building *walking up the street.*
> (correct) *Walking up the street,* I saw the Empire State Building.
> (incorrect) Mr. Brown bought a chocolate soda for the little girl *with whipped cream on top.*
> (correct) Mr. Brown bought a chocolate soda *with whipped cream on top* for the little girl.

Errors like those given above may be corrected in one of two ways: by rewriting the sentence so that the phrase will be close to the word it modifies, or by changing the phrase to a clause.

> (Misplaced and confusing) Take this pill *before going to bed* in a cup of warm milk.

(Correctly placed and clear) *Before going to bed,* take this pill in a cup of warm milk.

(Phrase to clause) *Before you go to bed,* take this pill in a cup of warm milk.

Practice 95

Rewrite each of the following sentences, in order to make them correct.

1. Smothered in gravy and onions, the waiter served the steak.
2. Filled with a hearty meal, the television set was turned on for an evening of entertainment.
3. At the age of three my father and mother took me out West.
4. We ate the pie that Mother baked in less than a minute.
5. Crossing the street, the car missed the pedestrian.
6. Miss Murphy bought a new suit for her nephew with a pin stripe.
7. Please take your suit coat to the tailor with the trousers.
8. Standing with propellers whirring, Mrs. Arthur was the last to board the plane.
9. Flying around the room, I saw two birds.
10. We saw a boat sitting on our front porch.

CLAUSES

A clause is a group of related words containing a subject and a verb, and any complements and modifiers. A clause may express a complete thought and be able to function independently as a sentence.

Bob ate the pie.

This kind of clause is called an **independent clause.** In many sentences, there are other clauses that depend on the independent or main clause to make their own meaning complete. This kind of a clause is called a **dependent,** or subordinate, clause. A dependent clause is joined to the main clause by a relative pronoun (such as *who, which,* or *that*) or by a subordinating conjunction (such as *after, although, as, because, if, before, since, unless, when, where,* and *why*).

Subordinate clauses offer the writer the chance to give more importance to an idea in the main clause by placing ideas of lesser importance in the subordinate clause. You will remember from your study of different kinds of sentences (pages 47–60) that this kind of sentence is called a complex sentence and that it may have one or more subordinate clauses. The complex sentence with its main and subordinate clauses permits the writer to arrange his ideas according to their relative importance. Notice the following examples.

Bob ate the cake *which Mary baked.*

The important idea here is *Bob ate the cake.* The fact that Mary baked it is only incidental to the main idea, and is therefore placed in a subordinate clause.

When the gates opened, the crowd entered.

Here, the interest centers on *the crowd entered. When the gates opened* only develops the main idea; thus, this secondary idea is placed in a subordinate clause.

Mary bought a new dress *after she had lost ten pounds.*

The clause *after she had lost ten pounds* is made subordinate because it is not as important as the main idea in this sentence. It is the task of the writer to decide which clause is to be made subordinate to another clause. Thus, in the first sentence, we might have had:

Mary baked the cake *which Bob ate.*

By subordinating one or another idea, the writer thus places the emphasis on the idea he feels is more important at that moment.

Practice 96

A. Locate the main and subordinate clauses in the following sentences. Label the S and V of each clause.

1. As soon as the game was over, the girls quickly headed for home.
2. We like to go on picnics when the weather is hot.
3. Before I do this problem, I would like to get some extra help.
4. Since Don has been at college, he has been studying very hard.
5. Although the captain of the team had a broken leg, he insisted on going to the game.
6. As soon as I was alone, I tried to ride my new bike.
7. Until the new house was finished, we lived with my aunt.
8. Since the dog belongs to a neighbor, I must be careful to treat it kindly.
9. When the car in front of her stopped, she slammed on her brakes.
10. After Mary had greeted Helen, the two girls boarded a plane for India.

B. Write ten sentences in which you place the important idea in the main clause, and the less important idea in the subordinate clause.

C. Write sentences in which the following clauses are used as subordinate clauses.

1. how they described the place
2. that it was terribly important
3. what the man wanted
4. why she never was asked
5. since I had found it in the first place
6. as we left the stadium
7. although she was very tired
8. if he really wanted to
9. after we left
10. because the reporter had made a mistake

The adjective clause. A subordinate clause may function as an adjective to modify a noun or pronoun.

The boy *who broke his arm* is my brother.

Here, the main clause is *The boy is my brother.* The subordinate clause, *who broke his arm,* is an adjective, modifying *boy.*

The relative pronouns, particularly *who, whom, which,* and *that,* join the subordinate adjective clause to the noun or pronoun it modifies. Sometimes the relative pronouns are called subordinators.

Practice 97

Copy the following sentences on a separate piece of paper. Underline the adjective clause in each sentence. Indicate the word it modifies.

1. Modern architects have designed homes that resemble those of the ancient Romans.
2. The cowboys of television have guns which always shoot straight.
3. The boy whom I saw was looking for a fight.
4. The gardener selected plants which would do well in shady spots.
5. Stagnant water contains germs which can do great harm.
6. In science we studied about fish that eat human beings.
7. When we went on our trip, we took a camera which was foolproof.
8. The Temple of the Sun was built in a field which is near Mexico City.
9. I do not know the name of the man who will take his place.
10. Modern man has invented machines that can do almost anything.
11. For the display at the garden club, we gathered stones that had moss on them.
12. The teacher gave a test that permitted students to use their books.
13. The native prepared a travois to carry his heavy burden to the trading post which was ten miles away.
14. The rivers were overflowing their banks because of the heavy rainfall which came in the spring.
15. From her window she could see the flowering dogwood tree which grew near the creek.

Punctuating an adjective clause sometimes gives trouble. Here is a rule to guide you.

If an adjective subordinate clause is not necessary to the meaning of the sentence, separate it from the rest of the sentence by a comma. Otherwise, no comma is needed.

> The scientist, *who taught at a small university in Ohio,* discovered a new element.

> The scientist's discovery is in a field *which is constantly being revolutionized.*

In the first sentence, the subordinate clause contains information which is not essential to a clear understanding of the main clause. In the second sentence, the information in the subordinate clause clarifies and completes the information presented in the main clause. The subordinate clause is essential to the main clause and should not be separated from the rest of the sentence.

Practice 98

Punctuate the following sentences with commas if the subordinate clause is not essential to an understanding of the main clause. If you have trouble deciding, read the sentence aloud. Note that occasionally a sentence can be read either way. You indicate by your punctuation which way you intend it to be read.

1. An old chisel which was probably used for engraving marble tablets turned up in the ruins.
2. Pandora found a box which she wanted to open.
3. The paper that I turned in to the teacher was lost.
4. Mr. Day who used to be a taxi driver is working at our school.
5. He made a report on *Kon Tiki* which is a wonderful tale of a great adventure.
6. Let Jim go to the store where the towels are for sale to buy some for all of us.
7. The principal knows many ways whereby he can find culprits.
8. It is not a good idea to start anything new on warm days when the class is suffering from spring fever.

9. The superintendent rose to make the announcement which everyone had been expecting.
10. Miss Klingman who teaches our homemaking courses has invited me to lunch.

The adverb clause. A subordinate clause may function like an adverb and modify a verb, an adjective, or another adverb. An adverb clause will tell where, when, how, under what conditions, how much, or why something happened, and often begins with a subordinating conjunction that connects the subordinate idea with the main clause.

Here is a list of the most frequently used subordinating conjunctions:

after	as though	in order that	that	whenever
although	because	provided	till	where
as, as if	before	since	unless	wherever
as long as	how	so that	until	whether
as soon as	if	than	when	while

Here are some examples of adverb clauses:

Louise swims *when the weather is warm.*

The clause *when the weather is warm* modifies *swims* and tells *time.*

Before you leave, put the chairs in order.

The clause *before you leave* modifies *put.*

The cake looks *as if it will be good.*

The clause *as if it will be good* modifies *looks* and tells *how* it looks.

Sara will sit *wherever there is a desk.*

The clause *wherever there is a desk* modifies *will sit* and tells *place.*

He went to Europe *so that he could consult a specialist.*

The clause *so that he could consult a specialist* modifies *went* and tells *why*.

Practice 99

A. Copy the following sentences on a separate piece of paper. Underline the adverb clauses. Indicate the word the clause modifies.

1. While you were away, the cat disappeared.
2. The dog follows wherever I go.
3. The old man looked as if he had lost his last friend.
4. The ironing must be done before we leave.
5. As soon as he finished, we left.
6. Marcia did not finish because the assignment was too long.
7. Since he has won a scholarship, he will be able to attend college.
8. He can go provided he returns before ten o'clock.
9. As soon as you are ready, we will leave.
10. He ate quickly lest he miss his train.

B. Copy the following sentences on a separate paper. Underline the subordinate clause in each sentence. Tell whether the clause is functioning as an adjective or an adverb. Indicate the word the clause modifies.

1. The man who walks with a limp is the custodian of our school.
2. When vacation comes, he polishes and waxes the floors.
3. The floors which he polishes are very slippery.
4. We all walk carefully lest we fall.
5. As soon as all the students come back to school, the floors lose their shine.
6. Taking care of a school which houses 1000 students is a big job.
7. The custodian must come to school very early when the weather is cold.
8. About three o'clock in the morning, he lights the big furnaces which heat our building.

9. Sometimes we get too warm and turn off the heaters until we cool off.
10. The custodian always appreciates a room which the students try to keep clean.
11. At the end of the day the custodian lowers the flag which flies from the pole in front of the school.
12. He folds it carefully before he puts it away.
13. He locks the school securely so that no one will break in.
14. When he has finished all his chores, he departs immediately for home.
15. The man who works as a custodian has a hard job.

The noun clause. A subordinate clause may function as a noun, and it may appear in a sentence in any one of the following important functions:

1. As the subject:
   Whatever you select will please me.
2. As the direct object:
   He noticed *that she had a beautiful smile.*
3. As the indirect object:
   Tell *whoever calls* the price.
4. As a subject complement:
   My request is *that you tell Mabel.*
5. As the object of a verbal:
   He has gone downtown to purchase *whatever he needs for the trip.*
6. As the object of a preposition:
   The length of our stay depends on *how much money we have.*
7. As an appositive:
   We found it hard to believe Donna's story *that she had found the watch.*

If you have trouble recognizing the noun clause, try substituting the word *it* for the clause, or the correct form of the pronoun *he* or *she,* if the clause refers to a person. In many cases, although not all, this test will work.

Practice 100

A. Copy the following sentences on a separate paper. Tell what important part of the sentence each clause is performing.

1. Whatever he says is humorous.
2. He wondered what he should do.
3. Tom told the legend that explained the sunrise.
4. The truth is that no one wanted to leave.
5. Ask whoever calls the way to the party.
6. Scientists have learned that smog contains gases from gasoline motors.
7. What he said to his mother upset her greatly.
8. Lake Louise is where I caught my largest fish.
9. His suggestion that we all contribute something met with general approval.
10. Try to learn whatever the teacher is explaining.

B. Rewrite the following sentences on a separate paper as one sentence by placing one idea in a clause that modifies the other idea.

1. Joe read the names. Mable recorded the scores.
2. The boy is our star pitcher. He is a good student.
3. His friend has left. Does Jim know that?
4. You must finish doing the assignment. Then you may read your book.
5. We don't know what he will say. It is a mystery.
6. I bought a new coat. I will wear it on my trip.
7. The highway is clearly marked on the map. We should take that highway.
8. Prepare a list of your clothes. They should be the ones that you wish to take with you.
9. Both my sister and I live in this town. My parents were married here.
10. You must be in your seats. Be there when the bell rings.

CHAPTER

Punctuation

All writing makes use of punctuation marks to separate words and sentences into easily understood groups. Without punctuation, writing becomes an unintelligible jumble of words. With too much punctuation, or with incorrectly placed punctuation, your writing may prevent the reader from understanding what you have said. With proper punctuation, your writing is easier to read and understand.

END PUNCTUATION MARKS

The marks used to punctuate the end of a sentence are the period, the question mark, and the exclamation point. The kind of sentence you have written will determine which of these you will use. The reader depends on the end punctuation to tell him how to read the sentence. You, the writer, are calling the signals; be sure you call the right ones.

The period. Use the period at the end of a sentence that makes a statement (*declarative*) or give a command (*imperative*).

> Declarative sentence: Tom broke his leg.
> Imperative sentence: Please shut the door.

209

The question mark. Use the question mark at the end of a sentence that asks a direct question. This kind of sentence is called an *interrogative* sentence.

> Did Tom break his leg?
> Tom broke his leg?

The exclamation point. Use the exclamation point at the end of a sentence that expresses strong emotion, such as surprise, fear, or disgust. This kind of sentence is called an *exclamatory* sentence.

An exclamation point is also used after an interjection that expresses strong emotion.

> Ugh! What a mess!
> Oh, fine! The tire is flat!

An exclamation point is used at the end of an imperative sentence that shows strong emotion.

> Run for your life!
> Go to bed at once!

Use exclamation points sparingly. A single exclamation point is all that is ever needed. In writing a short composition, especially, you will be wise to use few—if any—exclamation points.

Practice 101

A. Read the following sentences aloud as they are written and punctuated. Note how the end punctuation marks determine the way you read them.

1. Jenny is leaving.
2. Jenny is leaving?
3. Jenny is leaving!
4. Miss Phillips gave me an "A."
5. Miss Phillips gave me an "A"!
6. Miss Phillips gave me an "A"?
7. I passed?
8. I passed.
9. I passed!

B. Rewrite the following sentences. Use the end punctuation marks that are needed. Tell whether each sentence is declarative, exclamatory, imperative, or interrogative.

1. Did he leave
2. Flood waters covered the Ohio valley
3. Stop talking
4. Jenny, your friend is here
5. Where did the teacher go
6. We are leaving soon
7. The girls left for Oregon, where they will stay for a week
8. Can you walk a little faster
9. Phone Sue Martin as soon as you can
10. Put that yo-yo away now

C. Write a paragraph of several sentences. Use several different kinds of sentences needing different marks of punctuation.

Other uses of the period. Here are other uses of the period. Use the period after an abbreviation.

Mr.   lb.   ft.   U.S.A.   Dr.

Use the period as a decimal point, and to separate dollars and cents when you are writing amounts.

.58   .089 $50.86 $10.25

Practice 102

Rewrite the following letter. Insert periods wherever needed.

1809 Garden St
Oak Lawn, Ill
January 8, 19——

Dear Pete,

Mr Blackman wrote me that two weeks at his summer camp will cost $76 25 I was curious about the 25, and he explained that this was a key deposit

He said that Dr Foster will examine me on March 6 at

9:30 A M I hope I pass, because I'm really looking forward to going to camp with you

Yours truly,
Bob

INSIDE PUNCTUATION MARKS

The comma. Next to end punctuation marks, the comma is the most useful mark of punctuation for the writer and reader. It is the comma that helps both the writer and the reader to keep the meaning of the sentence clear.

> Mary the hairdresser is here.

Unless the writer uses punctuation in sentences like this one, the reader will not know who Mary is, or how to read the sentence. The placement of a comma will clarify the situation at once.

> Mary, the hairdresser is here.

Mary and the hairdresser are two different people.

> Mary, the hairdresser, is here.

Mary and the hairdresser are one and the same person.

You can understand, therefore, how important it is to know the correct use of the comma. Here are some rules to help you.

1. Use a comma to separate from the rest of the sentence words in direct address. These are words that tell to whom you are speaking.

> Mary, the hairdresser is here.
> Tell me, George, how are you feeling?
> Where did he go, John?

2. Use a comma to separate from the rest of the sentence a word or words that explain who or what someone or something is. These words are called *appositives* or appositive modifiers.

> Mary, the hairdresser, is here.
> Butch, my dog, chases birds.

Dr. John Stevenson, the pediatrician, is very popular with his patients.

The senator visited our principal, Mr. Davis.

3. Use a comma to separate words, phrases, or clauses in a series. The comma before the "and" that joins the last two items in the series may be omitted. Sometimes, however, it is needed to make your meaning absolutely clear.

Peter had soup, crackers, and cocoa for lunch. (Words in a series.)

The little rabbit hopped through the gate, down the hill, and across the meadow. (Phrases in a series.)

The vice-principal asked the new student who he was, where he lived, how old he was, and where he had studied previously. (Clauses in a series.)

4. Use a comma after an introductory subordinate clause or participial phrase at the beginning of the sentence.

When John was in Mexico, he attended a bullfight.

Although the soprano had a sore throat, she sang the aria beautifully.

These examples have clauses at the beginning.

Hampered by a heavy pack, Jim climbed the hill slowly.

Swimming furiously, he outdistanced the shark.

These examples have phrases at the beginning.

5. Use a comma to separate the exact words (direct discourse) of a speaker from the rest of the sentence.

Marjorie said, "Will you help me?"

"The president," said Mrs. Smart, "will now call the meeting to order."

6. Use a comma before the conjunction that links the independent clauses of a compound sentence.

The dads constructed the booths, and the mothers decorated them.

The boys gathered wood, and the girls set the table.
We wanted to visit Disneyland, but my cousins preferred
to see Marineland.

7. Use a comma to mark off thousands in large numbers.

5,082,364 men volunteered for duty.

Practice 103

Write these sentences on a separate piece of paper. Then put
punctuation marks where necessary in each of the sentences.

1. In case of fire houses will be protected
2. Dr Johnson my cat catches mice
3. The breakfast consisted of eggs and sausage orange juice
   toast and marmalade and coffee
4. By 1960 5000000 people had migrated to the new land
5. When it is raining hard buckets are not enough
6. While I was eating the telephone rang
7. The medical officers checked each man's blood pressure
   tested all reflexes listened to their hearts and checked
   pulse and respiration
8. While leaving Albert forgot his coat
9. How many *e*'s are there in *remembered*
10. When do we leave Walter

More comma rules. Here are some more rules to guide you
in the use of commas.

8. Use a comma to separate transitional words like "no," "yes,"
"however," and others when they appear at the beginning of the
sentence.

No, I will not help you.
However, the party was a success.
Yes, I can understand your problem.

9. Use a comma to separate the parts of dates and addresses.

Abraham Lincoln was born on February 12, 1809.
Jim lives at 2451 Sunnyvale Road, Springfield 3, Ohio.

10. Use a comma after the salutation in a friendly letter.

Dear Mary,
Dear Uncle George,

11. Use a comma after the closing of a letter.

Yours truly,
Sincerely yours,
As ever,

12. Use a comma to separate from the rest of a sentence parenthetical expressions, phrases, or clauses that can be omitted without changing the meaning of the sentence.

The pie, of course, is apple.
Mary will take Latin. This language is her choice, however, not mine.

In these sentences, the expressions "of course" and "however" are parenthetical, and are set off by commas.

The teacher, busy correcting papers, did not see the boy enter the room.

In the above sentence the parenthetical phrase, set off by commas, is "busy correcting papers."

Queen Elizabeth, *who is reigning monarch of England,* is a beautiful woman.
John Elson, *who came from Ohio,* was the first American to receive the award.

In these examples, the parenthetical clauses are set off by commas.

Practice 104

A. Write the following sentences on a separate piece of paper. Underline any parenthetical expression, and insert commas wherever they belong.

1. Our bird incidentally is eleven years old.

2. That book by the way will give you much valuable information about lobster fishing.
3. Ben despite his father's warning went to the circus.
4. You are after all your own boss and can do as you please about your course of study.
5. However I would choose wisely if I were you.
6. Most people as a matter of fact do not like to eat whale blubber.
7. The three children became as time went by more and more independent.
8. Pigeons you may be sure are not going to like living in a lion's den.
9. Your shoes if you don't mind my saying so need shining.
10. Honesty after all is said and done is still the best policy.

B. Rewrite the following story, inserting whatever punctuation is necessary.

Echo a beautiful maiden was punished by Hera the queen of the gods for interfering with her affairs. Her punishment a most unusual one was the loss of all power of speech except that of repeating only the last word that someone else had just spoken.

One day while walking with her friends through the forest Echo spied a handsome young man Narcissus. Although she immediately fell in love with him she was not able to speak to him but could only repeat his last word. Deeply unhappy that he did not return her love Echo wasted away gradually until there was nothing left but her voice mournfully repeating the last word of someone who had just spoken.

Today whenever we hear our voices echoing back from a cliff or from across a lake we may think of this tragic story from which we get our word *echo*.

The apostrophe. The apostrophe is a mark that is important in the spelling of possessives and the plurals of letters, figures, and numbers.

The correct use of the apostrophe is explained in the next chapter in the section on spelling. Consult the index for pages on which rules and exercises may be found.

Quotation marks. Writers use quotation marks for three purposes: to quote the exact words of a speaker; to give the title of a short story, poem, essay, song, or magazine article (but *not* the title of a book); and to set off a word or phrase for emphasis.

You will frequently use quotation marks when you write, whether you are writing a story, a bibliography for a report, or a letter to a friend about an article you read. In all these writing experiences, you will use quotation marks, and you should know how to use them correctly. Study the brief conversation that follows.

> John's mother said, "What do you boys want to eat?"
> "May we really have anything we want?" inquired John.
> "Today you may," replied his mother, "for it is your birthday."
> "Good," said John. "I choose liver, bacon, and spinach."

You may have observed that certain procedures must be followed when you are writing a conversation.

1. Use quotation marks before and after the words of the speaker.

> His mother answered, "John, your choice of food is rather unusual."

2. Unless the quotation begins the sentence, use a comma before the quotation to set it off from the rest of the sentence.

> The principal announced, "All seniors please report to the auditorium now."
> "All seniors please report to the auditorium now," announced the principal.

3. Place a comma (to mark the last word of the speaker) or end punctuation marks (period, question mark, exclamation point) inside the closing quotation marks.

"Will you get the paper?" asked father.

"What a relief!" sighed Mary.

"I don't think I'll be able to finish," groaned Sam, as he started on the second watermelon.

4. When a quotation is divided by the words that tell who is speaking, the second part begins with a small letter unless it is the first word of a new sentence.

"Joan will help you," said Mary, "when she has finished."

"I can't go," reported Bill. "My father is ill."

5. If a quotation consists of several sentences, put the last set of quotation marks after the last sentence.

"Can't you watch what you are doing?" screamed Sandra. "You have ruined my project that is due tomorrow. You are a clumsy oaf!"

"Sorry," murmured the awkward youth. "I merely wanted to borrow the ink. I didn't mean to upset it."

6. If a speaker talks for several paragraphs, we use quotation marks at the beginning of the paragraph to show that he is still speaking, but we do not use quotation marks at the end of the paragraph until he is finished.

Practice 105

A. Copy each of the following sentences, changing the punctuation marks in such a way as to change the speaker.

Mary said, "Hans is late."

(Rewritten) "Mary," said Hans, "is late."

1. My uncle said, "Mrs. Klim is going to visit us next week."
2. "Albert Peters," declared Sue Johnson, "is the best choice."
3. "Roger," asked Mr. Stubbs, "do you have my key?"
4. The teacher stated, "The principal will now address us."
5. "All right, Ricco," remarked Sandy, "tell us your side of the story."

B. Rewrite the following anecdote, adding punctuation wherever necessary.

They were a run behind with nobody out in the ninth inning Lucky Lucas the pitcher listened to the coach's instructions

Try to bunt toward first base he said and for Pete's sake don't pop it up in the air

Lucky tried to bunt on the first pitch To his horror he saw the ball pop straight up into the air As he grimly ran toward first base he saw that no one was covering the bag Lowering his head he tore around for second base as well and when no one stopped him he kept right on Seconds later as he headed for the plate he saw the ball rolling wildly past him toward the dugout

As Lucky headed back from home plate to the dugout he was met by the coach With a grin on his face the coach handed him his bat Foul ball he said

C. Write a conversation between yourself and a student who is new to your school. You are showing him around the school and introducing him to teachers and students.

The hyphen. The hyphen is a short dash used by writers either to indicate that parts of words have been separated, or to link parts of compound words. There are definite rules for its use.

1. Use a hyphen at the end of the line to show that you have divided a word. You should divide the word between syllables, as in *govern-ment, inter-national, presi-dent,* and *drug-gist.*

2. Do not divide words of only one syllable. Words such as *caught, hot, went,* or *cold* may not be divided.

3. Divide compound words between their main parts, as in *home-work, butter-cup, tread-mill.*

4. Divide prefixes and suffixes from the rest of the word: *enter-tain-ment, under-statement.*

5. Whenever possible, avoid dividing a word at the end of a

line. An uneven margin on the right hand edge of the page is preferable to a shower of hyphens.

Practice 106

Use a dictionary if necessary to learn where to divide each of these words. Copy the words, dividing them into syllables. Use a hyphen to separate the syllables. Remember not to separate words of one syllable.

1. January	11. end
2. American	12. affectionate
3. dachshund	13. airplane
4. furnace	14. butter
5. frankfurter	15. earthquake
6. enrollment	16. dessert
7. Christians	17. understanding
8. might	18. belittle
9. comprehension	19. rug
10. command	20. collie

Here are some further rules for the use of the hyphen.

6. Use a hyphen to link compound numbers from twenty-one to ninety-nine.

> The committee ordered twenty-six gallons of cider.

7. Use a hyphen to join parts of a compound word that consists of a noun and a prepositional phrase.

> son-in-law
> man-of-war

8. Use a hyphen to join the prefixes *ex* and *self* to the main part of a word.

> She was his ex-wife.
> Her self-sacrifice was commended.

Practice 107

Copy these sentences, adding hyphens wherever needed.

1. His father in law is self conscious.

2. My ex girl friend has thirty two cousins.
3. The president's daughter was the thirty fifth person to vote.
4. She is entirely self reliant.
5. My sister in law is a helpful person.

The colon. The colon is a formal mark of punctuation that has rather limited use. However, you should know when and how to use it.

1. Use a colon after the salutation of a business letter.

> Dear Sir:
> Gentlemen:

2. Use a colon before a list of items, especially after such expressions as "the following" or "as follows."

> When we visited the zoo, we saw the following animals: lions, tigers, zebras, elephants, and bears.
> He gave directions as follows: pack your bags, eat your breakfast, and be ready to leave by 7:15 A .M.

3. Use a colon to express hours and minutes in numbers.

> 7:15 P.M.
> 8:45 A.M.

Practice 108

Copy the following sentences inserting a colon wherever needed.

1. His train left at 901 P.M.
2. The farmer planted the following grains barley, oats, and rice.
3. The letter from the school principal to my father began, "Dear Sir."
4. I began my letter to the mail-order company, "To Whom It May Concern."
5. Our school closes at 320 P.M.

The semicolon. The word **semicolon** means "half-colon," and that's just what this mark of punctuation looks like (;). However, its use does not resemble that of the colon.

In use, the semicolon is more like a period or a comma, as it marks the separation of the independent clauses of a compound sentence. The semicolon is a stronger mark of separation than the comma, but not so strong as a period. It is used instead of a conjunction to separate the independent clauses in a compound sentence whenever the clauses are closely related in thought.

> John went to Minnesota to study, but Jim decided to join the Navy.
>
> Marjorie likes honey; I don't.

Practice 109

A. Write five compound sentences by combining two of these independent clauses in each sentence. Use a semicolon or a conjunction wherever needed, and add modifying words, phrases, and dependent clauses as you wish.

1. the rain stopped
2. Ed did not come
3. Joe was climbing a ladder
4. the dog barked
5. Bob felt ill
6. the train whistled
7. the neighbor screamed
8. I opened the windows
9. Sue was planting pansies
10. the air was hot

B. Insert a semicolon, a period, or a conjunction in the following sentences to clarify their meaning. Do not write in the book.

1. Answer the telephone please I'm bathing the baby.
2. Ross is basically kindhearted hence his actions yesterday are hard to explain.
3. This size is the one called for in the blueprint you may check with the original copy.
4. He recognized and waved at all his friends they in turn waved back at him.
5. Almost everything is prepared only the salad must still be tossed.
6. Act your age if you can't do so admit it.
7. To ask questions is reasonable but to refuse to follow instructions is not.
8. My taxi was stalled in traffic however I saw her just as she accepted the first prize.

9. This is not the way to work the problem Bud yet you seem to have the right answer.
10. Heather is a good student as a rule however she has trouble with examinations.

C. Rewrite the following sentences, punctuating them properly.

1. Albie tell the policeman what you saw
2. At that moment Mr. Loane the shop teacher walked through the door
3. Mother called Vivian will you please come to the telephone
4. I'd like to order a list of books including *Silas Marner The Red Badge of Courage* and *The Cruel Sea.*
5. On August 3 1941 at 715 PM the news was released to the residents of Schenectady New York
6. Just as you called Kathleen Lois Brad arrived
7. As soon as the schedule was posted many students came in to protest
8. Is this the key to your car the officer asked
9. Joan your wallet is in the principal's office said Esther
10. Have any of you seen the late movie *The Librarian's Dilemma*
11. At the head of the aisle Mr. Garber my history teacher stood with a large scroll in his hand
12. Every Tuesday Thursday and Saturday I visit my grandmother on Wentworth Street in Bronxville New York
13. Where have you been Glenn Mother asked
14. Only three desserts are listed on the menu tapioca pudding ginger ice cream and stewed prunes
15. Writing for the school newspaper a very important job is an assignment for the most talented students only
16. When will you finish your report Miss Wrangley asked
17. As soon as all the homework was completed Mother collapsed into an easy chair
18. I finished my homework early Thornie is still doing his however
19. Chuck Phoebe or you will be chosen at the next meeting
20. Do you Colin know the proper way to tie a bow tie asked the manager

CHAPTER *14*

Spelling and Capitalization

SPELLING

One of the most important skills to develop is the ability to spell words correctly. If you have ever tried to read a composition in which there are misspelled words, you know how difficult the task is. The person who reads your paper will get a lot more out of it if he can read it quickly and easily without having to stop to figure out incorrectly spelled words.

There are five basic steps to learning how to spell.

Hear the word. How does it begin? How does it end? Does it sometimes have another pronunciation? How many syllables has it? Does the sound of the word resemble the thing it names?

See the word. Take a good look at it. Study all its parts. Do you see the letters you heard when you listened to it? Are there silent letters in the word? Do you recognize prefixes and suffixes you have studied? (See pages 32–39.) Do you recognize the root? Are there special combinations of letters in the word? Are there double consonants or double vowels? Do you know other words that have the same root or the same prefixes and suffixes? Do you know other words that have the same sound but are spelled differently?

Say the word. Look the word up in the dictionary if you are not sure of its preferred pronunciation. Make use of the diacrit-

225

ical marks to study its sounds. Notice where the syllables divide, and then pronounce the word carefully, giving each syllable the required stress. Pronounce the beginning and ending letters carefully and distinctly.

Write the word. Practice writing the word, first by syllables, and then as a complete unit. Note the sequence of the letters. Where do the combinations of letters come? Does it have letters that extend above and below the line? Does it start with a capital letter? Does it contain letters that are part of the spelling but not of the sound? If it is a noun, do you know how to spell the plural? If it is a verb, does the spelling change in the *-ing* form or in the past tense?

Use the word. Study all its meanings. Make the word an active part of your speaking and writing vocabulary. Think of other words that mean about the same as this word and of other words that mean the opposite. How does this word differ from its synonyms? What part of speech is it? Can it function as other parts of speech?

There are several basic rules for improving your ability to spell correctly.

Proofread your papers for spelling errors. Allow time for proofreading even on a test.

Keep a list of your own spelling "demons," reviewing them as often as necessary to maintain a better recall of the way they are spelled.

Finally, write legibly so that the person who reads your paper can be sure of what you wrote.

A knowledge of the rules for spelling words will help you improve your spelling. For most rules of any sort, there are exceptions; spelling rules have their exceptions, too. Study both the rules and the exceptions.

General rules for spelling. 1. Words containing *ie* or *ei* generally follow the rules in this old rhyme:

> Use *i* before *e*
> Except after *c*
> Or when sounded as *a*
> In *neighbor* and *weigh*.

ei words		*cie* words
forfeit	leisure	financier
either	their	species
neither	height	
weird	foreign	
seize		

2. Drop a final silent *e* before adding a syllable that begins with a *vowel* (dine, dining), but keep the final silent *e* before adding a syllable that begins with a *consonant* (hope, hopeful).

3. Verbs that end in *ie* drop the *e* and change the *i* to *y* when *ing* is added.

die, dying   lie, lying   tie, tying

4. Words of one syllable that end in a consonant preceded by a single vowel double the consonant before a suffix beginning with a vowel.

mop + ed — mopped
swim + ing — swimming

In many cases, longer words that are accented on the final syllable and that end in a consonant preceded by a single vowel also double the consonant before a suffix beginning with a vowel.

confer + ed — conferred
regret + ing — regretting

5. Most adjectives that end in *y* preceded by a consonant change the *y* to *i* when a suffix is added.

lazy — lazily
busy — business

6. Verbs ending in *y* change spelling in the third person singular (he, she, it) form.
A *y* preceded by a vowel adds *s*.

I obey   he obeys   we enjoy   he enjoys

7. A *y* preceded by a consonant changes to *i* and adds *es*.

I copy   he copies   we fly   he flies

Practice 110

A. Add the missing letters, either *ie* or *ei*, to the following words:

1. p....ce
2. n....ther
3. dec....ve
4. s....ge
5. v....l

6. financ....r
7. fr....ght
8. cash....r
9. handkerch....f
10. misch....vous

B. Write the *ing, able,* or *ful* forms of these words:

1. lose
2. care
3. debate
4. grace
5. write

6. note
7. hope
8. believe
9. shame
10. force

11. come
12. use
13. solve
14. owe
15. desire

C. Write the *ing* form (present participle) and the *ed* form (past participle) for each of these verbs:

1. bat
2. beg
3. plan
4. stop
5. whip

6. file
7. hire
8. sun
9. drag
10. shine

Rules for spelling plurals. 1. Most nouns form plurals by adding *s* to the singular.

boy, boys   girl, girls

2. The plural forms of some nouns do not follow any rules:

ox, oxen
child, children
foot, feet
mouse, mice
datum, data
formula, formulas, or
    formulae

goose, geese
woman, women
man, men
axis, axes
basis, bases
locus, loci

3. Some nouns have the same form in the singular and in the plural.

    a. Some may be either singular or plural in meaning: *fish, sheep, trout, deer.*

    b. Some are always singular in meaning and take a singular verb: *measles, news, physics, civics.*
       Measles is a miserable disease.

    c. Some are always plural in meaning and take a plural verb: *spectacles, scissors, pliers, shears, trousers.*

       The scissors are on the table.

4. Nouns ending in *y* add *s* to form the plural when the *y* is preceded by a vowel.

      key, keys   day, days

5. Change *y* to *i* and add *es* when the *y* is preceded by a consonant.

      sky, skies   baby, babies

6. For compound words, or words combined with other words, make the most important word plural.

      father-in-law, fathers-in-law

7. Words combined with the suffix *ful* add *s* to the end of the word.

      cupful, cupfuls

8. Nouns that end in *f* or *fe* form plurals in several different ways.

    a. They may add *s* to form the plural.

      handkerchief, handkerchiefs
      safe, safes

    b. They may change *f* or *fe* to *ves.*

      calf, calves
      shelf, shelves

    c. They may use either form.

       scarf, scarfs, or scarves
       wharf, wharfs, or wharves

9. Nouns that end in *o* also form plurals in different ways.

    a. They add *s* if the word pertains to music.

       alto, altos

    b. They add *s* if the *o* is preceded by a vowel.
       rodeo, rodeos

    c. They add *es* in all other cases.
       tomato, tomatoes

10. Nouns that end in *s, ch, x, z,* or *sh* add *es* to form the plural.

       church, churches
       box, boxes
       bush, bushes

11. Letters, symbols, numerals, or words used as examples form the plural by adding an apostrophe and *s.*

       3's a's &'s to's

12. Proper nouns follow the general rules for forming plurals except that a name life Wolf or Berry will simply add *s.*

       Mr. and Mrs. Wolf, The Wolfs
       Mr. and Mrs. Adams, The Adamses

Practice 111

A. On the next page is a list of fifty words. Some are in the singular form and some in the plural. Supply the missing form.

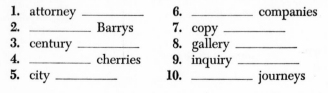

1.	attorney _____		**6.**	_____ companies
2.	_____ Barrys		**7.**	copy _____
3.	century _____		**8.**	gallery _____
4.	_____ cherries		**9.**	inquiry _____
5.	city _____		**10.**	_____ journeys

11. _____ ladies
12. _____ libraries
13. bacillus _____
14. Chinese _____
15. _____ volcanoes
16. baboon _____
17. proof _____
18. salmon _____
19. child _____
20. mouse _____
21. _____ teeth
22. knife _____
23. but _____
24. fox _____
25. scarf _____
26. x _____
27. auto _____
28. woman _____
29. wife _____
30. _____ leaves

31. series _____
32. monkey _____
33. Japanese _____
34. Negro _____
35. _____ pianos
36. woman shopper _____
37. go-between _____
38. board of education _____
39. and _____
40. tax _____
41. tie _____
42. datum _____
43. _____ lice
44. _____ kings
45. sheep _____
46. oasis _____
47. Christmas _____
48. man-of-war _____
49. class _____
50. cocker spaniel _____

B. For each of the nouns in the following list, compose two sentences—one to show its use as a singular word, and one to show its use as a plural word.

> boy, boys
> The boy is studying his lesson.
> The boys are playing football.

1. army
2. buffalo
3. deer
4. ox
5. tablespoonful
6. roof
7. cry
8. salary
9. shelf
10. 10

11. valley
12. looker-on
13. chicken
14. fox
15. fence
16. alto
17. tomato
18. grief
19. Negro
20. child

C. In the following sentences, write the plural form of the nouns in parentheses.

1. The (man) _____ bought two (knife) _____.
2. Several (wharf) _____ were constructed in the harbor.
3. The (fox) _____ were kept in a pen that was thirty (foot) _____ wide.
4. (Ox) _____ are important as beasts of burden.
5. The (president-elect) _____ conferred in the library.
6. The (mouse) _____ ate the cheese.
7. In many places, (deer) _____ do great harm to crops.
8. Next we will have two soprano (solo) _____.
9. The (potato) _____ should be kept in a cool, dark place.
10. Our allies have raised the (embargo) _____ on silver.

Spelling possessive nouns. The possessive form of a noun requires an apostrophe. There are, however, some rules for the use of the apostrophe.

To form the possessive of a singular noun, add 's.

> The boy's book was lost.
> Jenny's hair is curly.
> Gus's whiskers are long.

Occasionally, a singular noun ending in s will sound awkward if the apostrophe and s are used in forming the possessive. In such cases, the apostrophe only may be used, as in *Aristophanes'*, the name of a Greek dramatist. Generally, the apostrophe and s is preferred, however.

The formation of the possessive plural of a noun depends on the spelling of the plural.

1. If the plural form ends in s, add the apostrophe after the s.

> The boys' shirts were torn.
> The dogs' tails were short.

2. If the plural form does not end in *s*, add the apostrophe and *s*.

> The women's coats were cleaned.
> The children's toys broke.

No apostrophe is used in the possessive pronouns *its*, *hers*, *theirs*, and *ours*.

> The book is hers.
> The new car is ours.

Practice 112

A. For each of the words in the following list, give the possessive form.

1. salesman, salesmen
2. woman, women
3. company, companies
4. baby, babies
5. chairman, chairmen
6. army, armies
7. lady, ladies
8. child, children
9. ox, oxen
10. enemy, enemies

B. Write the following sentences on a separate piece of paper, adding apostrophes wherever necessary.

1. The childs wagon in Mr. Wilsons driveway is certainly not his.
2. Three companies are having picnics next week at Jim Steeles resort.
3. Several ladies dresses and mens suits were collected by womens clubs last week for the Red Cross.
4. The companys president called a salesmens meeting for next Tuesday.
5. The policemans duties included asking everyone for his drivers license.

6. A soldiers life is not an easy one, especially if he is in the front lines.
7. The blue jays shrieks warned us of the bobcats approach.
8. The bears tracks were not difficult for the expeditions leader to follow.
9. Tommys costume consisted of his fathers hat and cane.
10. A girls voice could be heard above the orchestras tuning.

Homonyms. Homonyms, words that sound the same but have different spellings, frequently cause spelling errors. A working knowledge of the correct spelling of some of the more confusing pairs will help you in your writing.

all ready: completely ready. We are *all ready* to leave.
already: previously, by now. He has registered *already*.

altar: a table for a religious ceremony. The priest placed his Bible on the *altar*.
alter: to change. He will *alter* his plans.

all together: everyone in the same place. We went to the show *all together*.
altogether: entirely. The price was *altogether* ridiculous.

brake: a device to check speed. When he parked his car, he set the *brake*.
break: to shatter. He tried not to *break* the dishes.

capital: a city. Sacramento is the *capital* of California.
capitol: a building. There is a dome on our *capitol*.

Practice 113

On a separate piece of paper, write the word that makes each of these sentences complete and correct.

1. The bride approached the (altar, alter).
2. He had no opportunity to (brake, break) training.
3. She wears (all together, altogether) too much jewelry.
4. The (capital, capitol) city was in flames.
5. Are you (all ready, already) to leave?

6. The (capital, capitol) was made of marble.
7. The (brake, break) on the bicycle did not work.
8. We did not (altar, alter) any of our plans.
9. We went to the show (all together, altogether).
10. He has completed his task (all ready, already).

More homonyms. Here are some more pairs of homonyms.

coarse: not fine. An Airedale has *coarse* hair.
course: a route. He followed the *course* of the river.

complement: something that completes. In the sentence "Marcia is chairman," *chairman* is a subject *complement*.
compliment: praise. The student received a *compliment* for his composition.

council: a lawmaking group. Jim attends Student *Council* meetings on Thursdays.
counsel: an attorney; advice. The teacher gave good *counsel*.
consul: a government representative. Lord Dunsday is the *consul* at Hong Kong.

desert: an arid region; to abandon. To *desert* the army in battle is both cowardly and criminal.
dessert: the last part of a meal. We will have pie for *dessert*.

forth: out from. The Indian went *forth* with a yell.
fourth: after third. John was *fourth* in line.

Practice 114

Copy the following sentences on a separate piece of paper. Use one of the homonyms in the group just preceding in each of the places where a word has been omitted.

1. Billy, you will be the _____ in line.
2. The pink scarf will _____ your outfit.
3. Ice cream makes a good _____.
4. The Student _____ will purchase the paint.
5. I will come, of _____.
6. The prisoner listened to the _____ of his priest.

7. The temperature in the _____ reaches 120° in August.
8. The _____ sand on the beach irritated my feet.
9. The animals went _____ from the ark.
10. "Thank you for the _____, kind sir," said Alice.

More homonyms. Here are five more troublesome pairs.

hear: listen to. "Can you *hear* the chimes?" said Mary.
here: in this place. "Not from *here*," replied her sister.

lead: a metal. *Lead* is used to make paint.
led: guided. The choir master *led* the singing.

passed: moved ahead. The Mercury easily *passed* the tractor.
past: time gone by. In the *past* the Egyptians worshiped cats.

peace: quiet order; absence of war. Many men want *peace*.
piece: a part of. "I'd like a *piece* of mince pie," said Mike.

plain: simple, homely. Jenny is a *plain* girl, but she has a radiant personality.
plane: a tool; an airplane; a flat surface. John purchased a *plane* before he flew to Rio.

Practice 115

Here are some sentences containing homonyms given in the last group. Write a sentence of your own for each of the other "twins."

1. He can not *hear* if he sits in back.
2. They were happy to forget the *past*.
3. At Christmas we hear the saying, "*Peace* on earth; good will toward men."
4. The *plane* taxied to a stop.
5. The fire marshal *led* the parade.

More homonyms. The following sets often cause trouble.

principal: main; the head of a school. The *principal* of a school must have high ideals.

principle: a rule of conduct. He acted on *principles* taught by his religion.

stationary: fixed, immovable. A telephone pole is *stationary*.
stationery: writing paper. She purchased special *stationery* for her letter.

their: belonging to them. *Their* car is blue and white.
there: in that place. It is *there* in the driveway.
they're: a contraction of "they are." *They're* planning a trip to Florida.

threw: tossed. The President *threw* out the first ball.
through: to pass from one side to another. Janice came *through* the doorway.

to: toward; also used as part of the infinitive of the verb. He wants to go *to* Rome.
too: more than enough; also. Mary ate *too* much cake.
two: the number after one. The Joneses have *two* cars.

Practice 116

Write the following sentences from dictation. Do not begin to write until you have heard the whole sentence.

1. The movie makers went to Stockholm to film the sets.
2. Honesty is a basic moral principle.
3. Have you seen their new car?
4. John carries two pairs of glasses.
5. "Over There" is the title of a song that became popular during World War I.
6. Mr. McAdam threw the ball to Jimmy.
7. The principal spoke at the assembly.
8. I wonder what they're doing.
9. The sultan walked through the garden.
10. The teacher was too busy to eat lunch.

More homonyms. Here is a final group.

weak: not strong. The race is to the strong, not to the *weak*.
week: seven days. At the end of the *week*, the jury went home.

weather: a condition of the atmosphere. We are having rainy *weather*.

whether: indicating an alternative. He did not say *whether* he would go. (Notice that these are not precise homonyms, as there is a slight difference in pronunciation.)

whole: entire. He ate the *whole* roast.
hole: an opening. *Holes* appear in the pavement after rain.

who's: a contraction of "who is." *Who's* going with me?
whose: "of whom." *Whose* coat is this?

your: "of you." *Your* tire is flat.
you're: contraction of "you are." *You're* a good student.

Practice 117

A. Copy the following sentences using the correct word from the list above.

1. Where is _____ tie, Jack?
2. Did you say _____ going?
3. Our neighbor was digging _____ for his fence.
4. The _____ in India is humid.
5. "_____ a great one to mess up the porch," scowled father.
6. Sunday is the first day of the _____.
7. Mabel did not know _____ umbrella she had.
8. Let me tell you the _____ story.
9. He did not know _____ to go.
10. The boy's leg was _____ after the plaster cast was removed.

B. Write ten sentences using the homonyms that cause you the most trouble. Read them to a friend and see how many he can write correctly.

USING CAPITAL LETTERS

A writer must know when and where to use a capital letter. A word that should be written with a capital letter is incorrectly spelled if it is written with a small letter. Similarly, a word that should be written with a small letter is incorrectly spelled if it is written with a capital letter.

There is a reason for the use of every capital letter. If you are in doubt, refer to an English grammar or to a dictionary in which rules for the use of capitals are given. Here are the main rules for using capital letters.

Proper nouns. A proper noun, naming a special person, place, or thing, is always capitalized.

> South Dakota   Jacques   Perth   Andersonville

A common noun names any one of a general group of persons, places, or things. Common nouns are not capitalized.

> state   boy   city

Names that particularize people. There are several rules governing the capitalization of people's names.

1. Capitalize the given names and family names of people.

> Bob met Sue and Mary Johnson.

2. Capitalize the word that shows family relationship when a name immediately follows it.

> On the porch sat Aunt Elizabeth.

3. Capitalize titles or abbreviations of titles that appear directly before a name.

> Dr. Brown and Professor Holmes conferred about the virus.

4. Capitalize titles that are used in place of a name in the sentence pattern.

> The Secretary of Labor spoke in Lakeport.

5. Capitalize abbreviations of titles or educational degrees after a name.

> Edward G. Loomis, M.D., has offices in the Franklin Building.

6. Capitalize the pronoun *I*.
7. Capitalize the names of special organizations of people.

> The Alethians met on Thursday.
> The Mormons built their new temple high on a hill.
> The Knights of Columbus installed their new officers.

8. Capitalize words that indicate the race and nationality of a person.

> French, Italian, Greek, and Negro leaders planned the celebration.

Practice 118

Copy the following sentences on a separate sheet of paper. Use capitals where needed.

1. One of the enlisted men escorted me into the tent and introduced me to major black.
2. The newspaper announced that mr. ralph cragmont was visiting his aunt, mrs. elsie hindmarsh.
3. The most popular professor is dr. tom crawford.
4. I would like to return to Europe to visit paris.
5. Neptune was god of the sea.
6. The car uncle dave was driving is owned by his friend, owen fath.
7. If you need a minister, the reverend donald curtis will be available.
8. John drake, a student at oak high school, has a brother named pete.
9. The queen of England is elizabeth, wife of philip, duke of edinburgh.
10. One of our greatest presidents, abraham lincoln, experienced defeat before he knew success.

Names for special places. Capitalize the names for special places. Here is a partial list:

> towns: Little Rock, New Orleans
> states: Ohio, West Virginia

countries: Switzerland, Denmark
rivers: Missouri, Seine
mountains: Allegheny, Sierra Nevada, Jura
streets: Emerson Street, Oxford Avenue, Twenty-third Street.
schools: Wenatchee High School, University of Nebraska
businesses: Macmillan Lumber Company
churches: First Baptist Church, Our Lady of Lourdes

Practice 119

Write a proper noun to match each of the common nouns in the list below. For example: school _____ Skyline High School.

ocean _____	river _____
city _____	state _____
county _____	building _____
church _____	mountain _____
continent _____	country _____
university _____	street _____
business _____	metropolis _____
library _____	district _____
station _____	section of the country _____

Names for special times. Such names are usually capitalized.

1. Capitalize the names of the days of the week, of the months of the year, but *not* of the seasons.

Friday   October   spring

2. Capitalize the names of holidays, famous events, documents, and periods.

Thanksgiving   the Declaration of Independence
the Dark Ages

Practice 120

Read the following sentences aloud. Tell where you think capital letters should be used, and give your reason.

1. School usually begins on the first monday in september.

2. We have our assemblies on wednesdays.
3. friday is test day at smithfield high.
4. School closes in june.
5. Our school closes for the christmas and easter holidays.
6. Some schools in europe have classes on saturdays.
7. The renaissance was the period of the rebirth of learning.
8. The war for independence was fought in the 1700's.
9. Airplanes were used in world war I.
10. The atomic age began in the twentieth century.

Other uses of capitals. Finally, there are some special rules to remember.

1. Capitalize religious terms.

   Bible   Catholic   Protestant

2. Capitalize the first word of every sentence.

   The clock struck one.

3. Capitalize the first word of every line of poetry.

   Twinkle, twinkle, little star,
   How I wonder what you are!

4. Capitalize the first word of a direct quotation.

   The doctors said, "You are in perfect health."

5. Capitalize the first word and all nouns in the salutation of a letter.

   Dear Margaret,
   My dear Melinda,

6. Capitalize the first word of a complimentary close.

   Yours truly,   Sincerely yours,   As ever,

7. Capitalize the names of school courses referring to a nation.

   French   Spanish   English   Latin

8. Capitalize the names of special courses.

   Education 101   U.S. History II   Chemistry I

However, do not capitalize the names of other courses in school, such as physical education, homemaking, social studies, or art, when they refer to general courses of study.

9. Capitalize the names of established school customs, traditions, cheers, and days.

> Tomorrow is the day of the Senior Picnic.
> The Awards Assembly will be held next week.

10. Capitalize names of books, poems, plays, articles, musical compositions, and art works. Do not capitalize prepositions or articles of less than four letters when they appear within a title, unless they are the first word.

> I was reading *Moby Dick*.
> Dickens wrote *A Tale of Two Cities*.

11. Capitalize points of the compass only when referring to specific regions, not direction.

> Sam lived in the West during the war years.
> We are going south for the holidays.

12. Capitalize each entry of an outline.

> I. Traffic problems in large cities
>   A. Problems caused by private cars

Practice 121

A. On a separate piece of paper, copy the following sentences, using capitals where necessary.

1. at mc chesney junior high school pete parker studied english, math, art, and social studies.
2. mother went south on the santa fe railroad and lived in the south all summer.
3. the bank of america is on broadway at twenty-fourth street and grand avenue in oakland, california.
4. for christmas mr. owens gave me a singer sewing machine and a copy of the *bible*.
5. after a year in commerce high school in san francisco, cali-

fornia, susan sporakis entered the high school in reno, nevada.
6. the topic of your composition today is what i want for christmas said the teacher.
7. the sacramento river empties into the pacific ocean.
8. this year thanksgiving came on november 27.
9. have the french assembly members voted on rearmament of west germany?
10. i saw the president of the united states in washington, d.c., on the steps of the white house.

B. Which words in the sentences should be capitalized?
1. one of the professors of music at williams college has just added a valuable stradivarius violin to his collection.
2. in twenty-five words or less, tell why you think our product, soggies, is better than any other cereal.
3. at senior awards night, our high school gives prizes for the best work in the fields of english, mathematics, and science.
4. sam graduated from midtown high school three years ago and has just returned to teach french and spanish.
5. the canada lynx is a dangerous animal that may attack hunters in the north woods.
6. european nations are prevented by the monroe doctrine from interfering in american affairs in this hemisphere.
7. some of the italian painters who lived during the renaissance did masterpieces that the world still admires.
8. "nevertheless," said mr. roberts, "the assignment to read seven pages of your history text should have been finished."
9. each spring, john and miriam headley used to go on a sailing cruise on the missouri river.
10. "while i nodded, nearly napping, suddenly there came a tapping,
as of someone gently rapping, rapping at my chamber door."

Practice 122

A. Here are the ten words most frequently misspelled by high school graduates in official examinations over the past ten years.

1. too	**4.** together	**7.** committee	**9.** separate
2. its	**5.** their	**8.** therefore	**10.** pleasant
3. believe	**6.** principal (chief)		

B. Mastery of the following list of frequently misspelled words may improve your spelling by as much as 40 or 50 per cent.

ache	different	loose	speech
across	dining	lose	stopped
all right	disappointed	losing	stretch
almost	doesn't	loving	studying
already	don't	meant	sure
animals	dropped	minute	surprise
another	enough	money	swimming
answer	finally	morning	taking
athletics	forty	necessary	than
babies	fourth	ninety	their
beautiful	friend	ninth	then
beginning	frightened	occasion	there
break	generally	piece	threw
business	getting	preferred	through
can't	government	prevent	toward
captain	grammar	principal	truly
certain	hoping	principle	until
children	interesting	probably	used
choose	intramural	quantity	usually
clothes	isn't	quiet	weather
coming	its	quite	whether
course	it's	really	whole
cousin	laboratory	receive	whose
definite	lady's	sandwich	won't
describe	laid	shining	wouldn't
description	led	similar	writing
didn't	library	sincerely	written

CHAPTER 15

Usage

You should observe correct patterns of usage in all your writing and speaking. Mastery of the patterns of usage of standard English will help you to write and speak clearly and accurately, and will improve your ability to communicate. Your audience includes teachers, fellow students, and all other persons who read what you write or hear what you say.

Standard English usage in the classroom may be different from that which you use in the schoolyard, or when casually talking. Also, patterns of usage vary with the message you are trying to communicate and the effect you are trying to create. Just as you wear one kind of clothing in cold weather and a different kind when you are in the tropics, you also use different patterns of writing for different situations. A formal report will contain patterns of usage different from the ones you would use in an informal note to a friend your age. If you are relating a conversation between two people who have no education, you will use certain colloquialisms and idioms that you would not use if you were reporting a conversation between two learned scientists. Your writing would be out of character if you used the same patterns in both compositions. You must use patterns of English that are suitable for the communication level of your composition. In general, however, the patterns of usage which make up standard English will be accepted as good writing and speaking form both inside the classroom and out.

In this chapter, you will study these standard English patterns of usage.

Words frequently misused or confused. Have you ever been confused about the correct use of two similar words? Here is a list of some of the more frequently confused pairs. Study them carefully so that you can use them easily and confidently.

accept–except

Accept means to take something that is offered to you.
Except usually means "other than" or "but."

> I accept your invitation.
> The boy accepted a ride home.
> Everyone went except Horace.

affect–effect

These are hard to keep straight because they are similar in spelling as well as in meaning.

Affect is generally a verb. It means the following: to move, to influence, to assume the appearance of.

> The death of my pet affected me deeply.
> He affected the swagger of a bully.

Effect functions as a noun and as a verb. As a noun it means the result or consequence, the accomplishment or fulfillment, or the impression.

> What effect did the medicine have on the patient?
> The change will take effect Monday.
> The actor wore sideburns for effect.

As a verb it means to accomplish, to bring about, or to make.

> The senator effected a change in the proposed bill.

aggravate–annoy

Aggravate means to make worse.
Annoy means to bother, anger, irritate.

Burning weeds will aggravate her hay fever.
Mother said, "Do not annoy me when I am ironing."

In informal speech *aggravate* is sometimes used to mean *annoy.*

The noise of the repair crew *aggravates* the old lady.

all right–alright

All right means all correct; there are no errors.
Alright is simply an incorrect spelling of all right; it doesn't mean anything.

"Your answers are all right," said the teacher.

almost–most

Almost means nearly.
Most means the largest part of.

He has lost almost fifty pounds.
He ate most of the pie.

already–all ready

Already means previously.
All ready means that all (things or people) are ready.

I have studied for the test already.
"Are you all ready to leave?" asked father as he picked up the last suitcase.

among–between

Among refers to more than two persons or things.
Between usually refers to two persons or things.

The cake was divided among the ten children.
This secret is just between you and me.

Note that *between* may refer to more than two in a sentence like the following: "A treaty was signed between the three powers." Also, you should use the objective form of the pronoun after these two words.

The king walked among *us.*
Let there be peace between you and *him.*

amount–number
> *Amount* refers to quantity (how much).
> *Number* refers to items that can be counted.

> The amount of homework appalled me.
> The number of pages assigned was ten.

Practice 123

Number your paper from 1–15. After each number write the word from the matching sentence that completes the sentence correctly.

1. Dandelions were growing (among, between) the wildflowers.
2. We were (already, all ready) to leave when the bell rang for a fire drill.
3. The steady drip of a leaky faucet (aggravates, annoys) me.
4. Jenny and Bill divided the responsibilities (among, between) them.
5. Bob is (almost, most) ten years old.
6. Mother said it was (alright, all right) to stay.
7. I cannot (accept, except) your invitation, Harry.
8. The weather was pleasant (accept, except) for a little rain.
9. A good haircut (affected, effected) a change in the student's appearance.
10. "The dentist has (most, almost) finished," said the nurse soothingly.
11. Spicy foods will (annoy, aggravate) stomach ulcers.
12. The police have thoroughly searched the suspect's house (all ready, already).
13. "I cannot (accept, except) your gift," said the policeman to the store owner.
14. Poe wrote a (number, amount) of short stories.
15. The balloons created a beautiful (affect, effect) at the dance.

More usage problems involving confusing pairs

beside–besides
Beside means next to, or close to.
Besides means in addition to.

> He walked beside Mary.
> Besides Harold, the group included Sam, Mike, and Perry.

borrow–lend
Borrow means to obtain something from someone on a temporary basis.
Lend means to let someone have something temporarily.

> I borrowed a dime from Miss Stokes today.
> She wanted to lend me a quarter, but I didn't need as much as that.

bring–take
Bring means to carry to the speaker.
Take means to carry away from the speaker.

> Sally, please bring me a note from your mother, explaining your absence.
> Stuart, take this book to the library.

can–may
Can expresses physical ability.
May implies permission.

> Can you do twenty push-ups without resting?
> May I leave the room?

farther–further
Both these words can refer to distance, but the word *further* may also be used to mean simply "additional."

> George swam farther than his cousin.
> I can give no further information.

formally–formerly
  Formally means in a formal or correct way.
  Formerly means previously, in the past.

  The girls were formally presented to society at the ball.
  Miss Irmegarde was formerly employed by the state.

funny–odd
  Funny means humorous.
  Odd means unique, different.

  Grandfather told a funny story.
  Aunt Elizabeth has an odd way of winking when she is talking.

healthful–healthy
  Healthful refers to something that is "full of health" for you.
  Healthy describes a person who is in good health.

  Raw carrots are healthful.
  A healthy mind means a healthy body.

learn–teach
  Learn means to acquire knowledge.
  Teach means to impart knowledge.

  I am going to learn to speak Russian.
  Mr. Zalenkov will teach the class.

leave–let
  Leave means to depart.
  Let means to permit.

  If you do not let me buy a Jaguar, I shall leave.

Practice 124

Number 1–20 on a separate paper. Beside each number write the word that makes each sentence complete and correct.

1. The little dog sat (beside, besides) her master all night.
2. Babe Ruth could hit a ball (farther, further) than anyone else.
3. Heins wanted to (borrow, lend) ten dollars.

4. Geraldine (can, may) run fast.
5. (Bring, Take) your report cards home tonight.
6. Grimes was (formerly, formally) installed as president.
7. Jake failed when he tried to (learn, teach) Marnie to swim.
8. Will your mother (let, leave) you join us?
9. Just before I sneezed, I had a(n) (funny, odd) pain.
10. The president said, "I have no (farther, further) information."
11. Thelma looks (healthy, healthful) again.
12. (Can, May) I have your attention?
13. When you come to class tomorrow, (bring, take) your spellers.
14. Please (borrow, lend) me your pen.
15. Jason was (formerly, formally) a captain.
16. He had to (leave, let) early.
17. The comedian was naturally (odd, funny).
18. How many will attend (beside, besides) you?
19. Jim was (learned, taught) by Joan.
20. Beet tops are very (healthy, healthful).

More usage problems

actual fact–honest truth

Both of these combinations illustrate the unnecessary use of an adjective to emphasize a noun that is strong enough to stand alone. A fact is actual; how can it be otherwise? The truth is honest; there is no other variety.

and–etc., etc.

The abbreviation etc. comes from two Latin words *et* and *cetera*. When translated, these words mean "and so forth" or "and others." In formal writing, this abbreviation should be avoided. The phrase "and et cetera" is of course never correct.

(Poor usage) He studied the following languages: Latin, Sanskrit, French, etc.

(Revised) He studied Latin, Sanskrit, French, and other languages.

like–as–as if
Like is generally followed by a noun or pronoun.
As if is followed by a clause.

> The girl looks like her father.
> It looks as if it will snow.

Use "*As* I say," not "*Like* I say" in formal English.

meanwhile–in the meantime
These words are used interchangeably. But "in the mean-*while*" is never used in formal English.

> Meanwhile, the house burned.
> In the meantime, the house burned.

neither . . . nor–either . . . or
The words in these pairs appear together.

> Neither rain nor snow stops the United States mail.
> Either do your homework properly or not at all.

real–very
Real means genuine.
Very is an intensifier used with adjectives and adverbs.

> Crane gave Martha a real diamond bracelet.
> Martha was very much impressed.

reason is because
The best way to handle this problem is to avoid it. Rephrase your sentence to eliminate this construction.

> (Awkward) The reason I can't swim is because I didn't learn early.
> (Revised) I can't swim because I didn't learn early.

think–guess
Think implies careful consideration of the facts of a problem.
Guess implies a spur-of-the-moment estimation.

> Did you think about my suggestion?
> Can you guess how many beans are in this bottle?

this here–that there
The words *this* and *that* are sufficient. Eliminate *here* and

there. The word *this* implies that something is close to the speaker. The word *that* implies that something is at a distance from the speaker. The adverbs are unnecessary.

too–to–two
> *Too* is an adverb and means "more than enough," or "also." It does *not mean* "very."
> *To* is a preposition.
> *Two* is an adjective.

>> The two suitcases are not too heavy for Gerald to carry.
>> He can take the umbrella, too.

want in–want out
> Improper usage. Say "want to come in," or "want to go out."

where at
> The "at" is unnecessary. Use *where* by itself.

>> Where is he?

who–which
> *Who* refers to persons.
> *Which* refers to things.

>> The man who called me was my doctor.
>> He wondered which (cookie) to choose.

Practice 125

Number your paper from 1–15. Beside each number write the word that makes each sentence complete and correct.

1. Can you untie (this, this here) knot?
2. The little boy ate (to, too, two) many Easter eggs.
3. Geraldine looks (like, as if) her cousin.
4. The book (who, which) is on the table is mine.
5. Spotty Anne (wants in, wants to come in).
6. I had a (real, very) good time.
7. The rat (thought, guessed) which door led to the cheese.
8. The (to, too, two) girls crossed Fifth Avenue.
9. It looks (as if, like) it will rain.
10. The physician was (real, very) tired after the operation.

11. Do you know (who, which) was elected?
12. He went (to, too, two) Hoboken.
13. Where did you find (that, that there) ball?
14. The astronaut (wanted out, wanted to get out).
15. I (think, guess) I will look at television.

Idiomatic use of prepositions. Particular prepositions are used after certain verbs, participles, adjectives, and nouns. Having good usage habits includes knowledge of the correct preposition to use. Here is a list of some frequently used combinations:

accuse of (a crime)
acquit of (all wrong-doing)
adhere to (one's decision)
agree to (a plan of action)
agree with (someone)
agreeable to (the offer)
angry at (the insinuation)
angry with (someone)
apply (oneself) to (the job or problem at hand)
argue for (a new trial)
argue with (someone)
believe in (someone or something)
capable of (any action)
compare to (anything, for illustration)
compare with (something, as an example)
concentrate on (the task)
concern for (her health)
concern in (a matter, i.e., interested)
concern with (his job, i.e., involved)
desire for (fair treatment)
desirous of (helping others)
devoid of (facial expression)

differ from (something else)
differ in (ideas)
differ with (someone else)
different from (that way, i.e., comparison)
disagree with (someone)
disapprove of (something done)
distaste for (idle chatter)
eager for (information)
empty of (its contents)
expert in (many fields)
foreign to (a way of life)
guard against (straining your eyes)
hint at (the answer)
independent of (something else)
infer from (a statement)
inseparable from (someone else)
interest in (the course of events)
jealous of (another's prosperity)
meet with (opposition)
obedient to (his command)
pertain to (another matter)
preparatory to (serving dinner)
prior to (going to bed)

profit by (experience)
prohibit from (leaving early)
protest against (unjust taxation)
reason with (a stubborn child)
refrain from (talking too much)
regret for (one's actions)
sensitive to (criticism)
separate from (the rest of the group)

sick of (his complaining so much)
sick with (pneumonia)
sympathize with (your ideas)
tamper with (the plant's machinery)
unworthy of (praise)

Practice 126

Write the following sentences on a separate piece of paper, inserting the proper prepositions.

1. He was obedient _____ his mother's slightest desire.
2. How does my answer differ _____ your answer?
3. I don't think you are capable _____ climbing that mountain.
4. He is too concerned _____ his own health to be properly concerned _____ his job.
5. My father has prohibited me _____ going out tonight.
6. I'm afraid I cannot sympathize _____ your purpose in asking for money.
7. "Why are you angry _____ me?" asked Laurie.
8. If you compare this copy _____ the original painting, you can see the difference.
9. Will you agree _____ my going to see the manager?
10. For ten days he was in bed, sick _____ a virus infection.

Double negatives. The negative words which follow do not require the presence of *no* or *not* in the predicate. Use them singly, avoiding the double negative.

never	no one	hardly
only	nothing	scarcely
none	neither	barely
nobody	nowhere	but (meaning only)

There are three kinds of usage problems connected with double negatives.

The use of a double negative for extra emphasis is one kind.

> (Incorrect) I never told nobody.
> (Correct)   I told nobody.
>   I never told anybody.

The use of concealed negatives creates a double negative effect.

> (Incorrect) I can't hardly move.
> (Correct)   I can hardly move.

The use of a double negative is permissible if the writer intends one negative to cancel out the other.

> A ride in a jet is not uncomfortable.
> Melinda was not unattractive.

Practice 127

On a separate paper number from 1–15. Beside each number write the word that makes the sentence complete and correct.

1. Ben couldn't hear (anything, nothing).
2. The teacher (can, can't) scarcely tell the twins apart.
3. The prizefighter hardly had time to land (any, no) punches.
4. The stain (was, wasn't) hardly seen.
5. Sutter was so surprised he (could, couldn't) scarcely speak.
6. Didn't you hear (anything, nothing)?
7. We couldn't hear the birds (anywhere, nowhere).
8. Sam didn't eat (neither, either) dessert.
9. Sue didn't see (anyone, no one) at the library.
10. The Smiths were not (happy, unhappy) to leave the stalled train.
11. Her report was (anything, nothing) but encouraging.
12. Jenny had never seen (no, any) rodeos.
13. The bull fight (was, wasn't) hardly amusing.
14. The rumor of his treason was not (founded, unfounded).
15. They never told (no one, anyone) about it.

CHAPTER *16*

Using the Library

The library is a storehouse of many different kinds of books. It contains not only books that you read just for knowledge or pleasure, but also books that you will wish to consult for specific information, that is, reference books. As you proceed through high school, you will make more and more use of these sources of information. You should learn early how to use the library and the reference books with ease and success. One great difference between an educated and an uneducated person is that the educated person knows how to find out things he does not know.

GETTING ACQUAINTED WITH THE LIBRARY

Probably the first step to take in learning to use the library successfully is to get acquainted with the particular library you use. Study the arrangement of the books and the location of the library equipment. What reference books does it have and where are they located? Where will you find the fiction books? Are recently published books displayed on a special shelf? What magazines and newspapers are available? Does the library have pictures and records that can be borrowed? Where do you check out books? Where do you return books? Get acquainted with the librarian, also. She is the "spark plug" of the library.

The next step is to learn how and when you may use the library and take out the books. What are the rules governing

the borrowing of books? What are the library's opening and closing times? Are there special schedules for holidays? How can you
get a library card? How many books may you take out at one
time? What are the regulations concerning losses or damage?
What fines, if any, are imposed for overdue books? You will learn
the answers to some of these questions through experience, but
you can learn the answers to many of them by reading the
notices that are posted around the library.

THE CARD CATALOG

When you feel that you have oriented yourself to the library,
take the next step of learning about the most helpful tool of all,
the card catalog. The card catalog contains three cards for each
book in the library: an author card, a title card, and a subject
card. Each of these cards contains all the information about a
book, but presented in a different order. The author card gives
the author's name on the first line; the title card gives the title of
the book on the first line; the subject card gives the subject on
the first line. All cards are arranged alphabetically.

Author card. The author's name appears on the first line, the
last name first. If the book is compiled or edited by the person
mentioned on the first line, "ed." or "comp." will be written after
the name.

Dates of the birth and death of the author are given if they
are known.

The second line is indented and contains the title of the book.
It is customary to capitalize the first word of the title and leave
the other words uncapitalized except for proper nouns. Additional information found on the title page of the book will follow
immediately after the title (name of illustrator, joint authors).
Next we find the *imprint:* the city where the publisher is located,
the publisher, the year of publication, or the copyright date. If
the copyright date is given, a © will often be written before
the year thus, © 1962.

The line on which the *collation* (the description of the physical and technical features of the book) is written is also in-

dented. The total number of pages is written in an abbreviated manner: 86p. If the book has maps, a frontispiece, illustrations, or plates, these facts will also be noted.

The *call number,* the number used to identify the book and its location in the library, is always found in the upper left hand margin of the card.

At the bottom of the card, you will see other information which is used only by the librarian.

821.08   Auslander, Joseph, 1897–   comp.
A   Winged horse anthology, by Joseph Auslander and Frank Ernest Hill. Doubleday 1929.
xxxi, 669p.

Title card. The title card is identical with the author card, except that the title is found both on the first line and in its usual place on the indented line below the author's name.

Winged horse anthology.
821.08   Auslander, Joseph, 1897–   comp.
A   Winged horse anthology, by Joseph Auslander and Frank Ernest Hill. Doubleday 1929.
xxxi, 669 p.

Subject card. The subject card is identical with the author card, except that the subject of the book is written on the first line of the card. It is possible to have more than one subject card for a book, since many books involve several subject areas.

AMERICAN POETRY—COLLECTIONS
821.08   Auslander, Joseph, 1897–   comp.
A   Winged horse anthology, by Joseph Auslander and Frank Ernest Hill. Doubleday 1929.
xxxi, 669p.

Other cards. A cross reference card refers you to another card where the subject or author that you want is handled under another heading. There are two types of cross reference: "see" and "see also."

A "see" reference is a reference from a heading which is not used in the catalog to a heading that is used.

```
+-----------------------------------------------------------+
|                                                           |
|                        CARS                               |
|                         see                               |
|                     AUTOMOBILES                           |
|                                                           |
+-----------------------------------------------------------+
```

A "see also" reference card is filed at the end of a group of cards with the same subject heading. The "see also" reference suggests other headings that might be useful.

```
+-----------------------------------------------------------+
|                                                           |
|                     NEWSPAPERS                            |
|                       see also                            |
|                     JOURNALISM                            |
|                                                           |
+-----------------------------------------------------------+
```

Guide cards project above the other cards in the trays of the card catalog. Each guide card has a subject or author written on it and serves as an aid in finding a desired place or heading in the catalog. For example, a book on *atoms,* if there is no guide card specifically for that subject, could be found between the guide cards for *ants* and *automobiles.*

Arrangement of cards in the catalog. Cards are filed alphabetically according to the words on the top line of each card. There are two methods of alphabetizing: word by word, and letter by letter. In the card catalog, alphabetizing is done word by word. For example, *antarctic* comes before *ant men.*

When the first word of the title of a book is an article (*a, an,* or *the*), the card is filed according to the second word. For example, *A Night to Remember* is filed under "N."

When the same word serves for a person, place, subject, and title, the order is: person, place, subject, title.

Buffalo, William
Buffalo, N. Y.
Buffalo, American
Buffalo Bill's Wild West Show

Abbreviations are arranged as though they were spelled out in full (except Mr. and Mrs.). *St.* is filed as saint; *Dr.* is filed as doctor.

Titles beginning with numerals are arranged in the catalog as if the numerals were written out. (100 would be filed as *one hundred.*)

All the cards for one author are filed alphabetically by the name of the author. A number of books by the same author are listed alphabetically by title.

Stevenson, Robert Louis
David Balfour

---

comes before

Stevenson, Robert Louis
Treasure Island

Names such as McBride, McGraw, and McSweeney are filed as if they were spelled MacBride, MacGraw, and MacSweeney.

Cards with the same subject are filed in alphabetical order by author.

ASTRONOMY
Adler, Irving
    The stars: stepping stones into space

---

comes before

> ASTRONOMY
> Baker, Robert Horace
> Introducing the constellations

Practice 128

A. Prepare author cards, title cards, and subject cards for the following well-known books. Use the copies of the books in your library to obtain all the information needed.

> Benary-Isbert, Margot, *The Ark*
> Eaton, Jeanette, *Narcissa Whitman*
> Verne, Jules, *Around the World in Eighty Days*
> Post, Emily, *Etiquette*
> Danzig, Allison, *History of American Football*

B. Draw a plan of the library in your school or town and show the location of fiction, nonfiction, and reference books, as well as the location of the card catalog and check-out desk. Write the five most important rules for the use of the library. Explain how these rules make the library a more pleasant place for everybody.

C. Look up each of the following topics, check the card catalog, and list three related books for each, as they are, listed in the card catalog you use.

> Radar equipment   Acting
> Sport cars   Fishing
> Lincoln, Abraham

THE DEWEY DECIMAL SYSTEM

The most widely used method of classifying books is known as the Dewey Decimal System, developed by Melvil Dewey (1851–1931) in 1876. There are also other systems, including the Library of Congress system, which is used in large libraries throughout the country.

By the Dewey system, books are classified into ten main groups.

000–099   General Works (encyclopedias, bibliographies, periodicals)
100–199   Philosophy (psychology, ethics)
200–299   Religion, Mythology
300–399   Social Sciences (government, education, folklore, customs, transportation)
400–499   Language (dictionaries, grammar)
500–599   Pure Science (mathematics, astronomy, physics, chemistry)
600–699   Applied Science (medicine, health, engineering, home economics)
700–799   Arts, Recreation (music, painting, dance, theater, sports)
800–899   Literature (poetry, drama, short stories)
900–999   History, Geography, Biography, Travel

Within each of these ten main divisions there are ten subdivisions. Let us take the 500–599 division, for example.

500   General Science
510   Mathematics
520   Astronomy
530   Physics
540   Chemistry
550   Earth Sciences
560   Paleontology
570   Biological Sciences
580   Botany
590   Zoology

In turn, each of these is subdivided further. Thus, the numbers from 520–529 (Astronomy) represent specific subjects in the field of astronomy.

520   General Astronomy
521   Celestial Dynamics

522   Spherical and Practical Astronomy
523   Descriptive Astronomy, Astrophysics
524   Astronomical maps and tables
525   Earth
526   Geodesy
527   Nautical Astronomy
528   Nautical almanacs, Ephemerides
529   Time measurements

Even these subdivisions can be broken down to a finer classification. When the classification becomes very fine, decimals are used. This use of decimals gave the system its name.

523   Descriptive Astronomy
523.1   Universe
523.2   Solar System
523.3   Moon

The classification number, or class number, is written on the back, or spine, of the book.

The call number.   Because the library will often have several books with the same class number, it is customary to arrange all books with the same number in alphabetical order by author. Large libraries will assign to each book a letter and number representing the spelling of the author's last name. This letter and number combination is called the *book number.* Small libraries, such as those in schools, use only the letter standing for the author's name. This letter is written below the class number on the spine of the book. The combination of the class number and the book number is known as the *call number.* It is so named because it is the symbol by which we "call" for a book we want.

Dewey's plan accounted for both fiction and nonfiction. Fiction means a story about an imaginary person, place, or thing. Nonfiction books are based on fact. He arranged for fiction books to be given numbers in the 800–899 division. Many libraries, however, use a simplified system for fiction. The fiction is arranged in one place alphabetically by the author's last name, with the first two letters of the author's last name used as the "call number."

   Cl   Cleary, Beverly
          Fifteen; illus. by Joe and Beth Krush. Morrow,
          1956

Arrangement of books on the shelves. The books are arranged on the shelves according to strict numeral order: 946; 946.08; 946.7.

The letter "R" on the line above the class number on the spine of the book indicates that the book is shelved in the reference section of the library.

Practice 129

A. Write the title and author of one book in your library for each of the following call numbers:

940.56	325.8	525.6
R	M	S

B. Use the card catalog to locate a book on one of the following topics. Write the author's name, title of the book, and call number of the book.

1. The bee
2. The French Revolution
3. Radium
4. Louis Pasteur
5. Early trade routes to the Orient

PARTS OF A BOOK

Learn the parts of a book in order to be able to use it intelligently. Here are the parts of a book in the order in which they usually appear:

Frontispiece, an illustration facing the title page of a book.
Title page, a page at the beginning of a volume that indicates the author, publisher, and place and date of publication.

On the reverse side appears the copyright information.

Dedication, an inscription dedicating a book to someone.

Preface, Foreword, or *Introduction,* material given at the beginning of a book to introduce it to the reader; it is usually written by the author or editor of the book. A preface or foreword is a somewhat informal statement to the reader; an introduction is a more formal preliminary statement or guide to the book.

Acknowledgments, a section in which the author or publisher acknowledges help received from certain people or other sources. Sometimes the acknowledgments are included in the preface.

Table of Contents, the part of the book which lists the chapter headings of the book with their page numbers in the order in which they come.

List of Illustrations, a list of illustrations with their page numbers in the order in which they come. This list usually comes after the table of contents. A list of maps and charts is sometimes given as well.

Text or Body, the main part of the book, beginning with the first page of the first chapter and ending with the last page of the last chapter.

Bibliography, a list of books or articles used as sources for the book, or suggested for further reading. Sometimes a bibliography is put at the end of each chapter, and at other times it can be found at the back of the book.

Appendix, a section of the book, coming after the body, that gives additional useful information. The appendix usually consists of notes, charts, and bibliographies.

Index, a section that gives in alphabetical order all the topics in the book and the exact pages for them; the index is usually found at the back of the book.

CARE OF A BOOK

Use a piece of paper for a bookmark; never use anything thicker. Do not keep papers inside a book, since the binding will be strained.

Cover textbooks to protect them from soil and weather.

Handle books with clean hands.

Never open a new book roughly. To open a book for the first time, follow these steps:

Lay the book on its spine, on a table or desk, then press the front and back covers down, holding the pages upright in one hand.

Press down a few pages at the back of the book and run your finger along the inside edge of the topmost page.

Repeat this procedure a few pages at a time in front and back until you have gone through the entire book.

REFERENCE BOOKS

The dictionary. There are two types of dictionaries, abridged and unabridged (see pages 26–27). The abridged is shortened; it leaves out many words and much information about words. The unabridged dictionary is as complete as possible, and contains most of the words of the English language. A small desk dictionary is an example of an abridged dictionary. *Webster's New International Dictionary, Third Edition,* is an example of an unabridged dictionary.

Webster's New International Dictionary has three main sections: the introductory section, the body, and the appendix.

In addition to the table of contents, and a list of plates, the introductory section in front of the dictionary contains the following parts:

Rules and Explanations, a section giving rules for spelling and explanations of the sounds of the English language.

History of the English language.

Addenda, a section containing new words recently added to the language.

Abbreviations used in the dictionary.

The greater part of the dictionary, of course, gives the words, their pronunciation, their derivation, and definition. In most dictionaries, definitions are given with the oldest use listed first. In the *New International,* each page of the main section is divided into two parts by a horizontal line. Above the line are the commonly used words, and proper names of characters in literature. Below the line are less common words, reformed spellings, less important Biblical proper names, and foreign words and phrases. Usually, the lower part occupies only a small fraction of the total page.

The appendix contains much useful information, such as the following:

Abbreviations used in writing and printing.

Signs and symbols.

Forms of address, a section that gives correct forms for oral and written address.

Pronouncing Gazetteer, a geographical dictionary.

Pronouncing Biographical Dictionary, a part that gives very brief descriptions of people of historical importance.

The encyclopedia.   Next to the dictionary, the encyclopedia is perhaps the most useful reference book in the library. Encyclopedias contain factual, often illustrated, descriptions of important ideas, people, historical events, and a host of other important items.

Encyclopedias are often published on two levels: as standard reference works, and as special references edited especially for schools and young people. Some of the most commonly used encyclopedias are listed here.

Standard Encyclopedias:
   Encyclopaedia Britannica
   Encyclopedia Americana
   Columbia Encyclopedia (one volume)
   Collier's Encyclopedia
Encyclopedias for young people:
   Britannica Junior
   Compton's Pictured Encyclopedia
   World Book Encyclopedia
   Book of Knowledge
   Our Wonderful World

Most encyclopedias are in alphabetical order, but a few are not. Some have signed articles. (In this case, the initials of the specialist who wrote the article appear at the end of the article. The initials are explained at the front of the first volume of the set.)

In order to keep up to date, some encyclopedias add a year-book each year; others practice the policy of "continuous revision," in that they revise some portion of the set each year. You should always be sure to check the copyright date of the volume you are using.

There are several helpful things to remember when using an encyclopedia or a set of encyclopedias.

If you do not find an article on the topic for which you are looking, use the general index.

Abbreviations are treated as if they were written out in full: *Mt.* as Mount; *St.* as Saint.

People are generally listed under their last names. However, saints, kings, and queens are listed under their given names: King *George* IV, Saint *Francis.*

If a subject has two or more words, you should look under the first word: *South* America.

Volume and page numbers, when given in indexes, are written in one of two ways: with a letter for the volume, followed by a number for the page (B–405); with a number for the volume, and a number for the page (14–7348).

Sometimes you'll notice that in the indexes of some encyclopedias there is a small letter after the page number: *a, b, c,* or *d.* Each page of the encyclopedia is divided into four parts and each part is indicated by one of these four letters. This device helps you to save time in locating information.

a   c

b   d

The World Almanac. This annual is published on January 1 each year, and is valuable for concise, up-to-date information (including statistics) on a wide range of subjects. The index is in the front of the book immediately following the table of contents. This index is indispensable because the information in the body of the book is not arranged in alphabetical order. It is important to remember that the date written on the book stands for the year the book was published and for which it was intended to be used. The information inside is up-to-date only as far as the year preceding the year of publication.

Practice 130

A. Make use of the unabridged dictionary, an encyclopedia, or an almanac to locate the following information:

1. The length of the Great Salt Lake
2. The use of nitrogen in agriculture
3. The shot-put record made by Zybina in 1954
4. A record of Daniel Webster's political activities
5. A picture of the tattooing on the face of a Maori chief
6. The address of the National Association of Letter Carriers
7. An alternate spelling for *theater*
8. A chart of the world's leading gold countries
9. The provisions of Article 58 of the United Nations Charter
10. An explanation of the Smith-Hughes Act

B. Select one of the following topics. Compare the information about this topic given in each of the reference books mentioned above, pages 269–272.

1. The Seven Wonders of the Ancient World
2. The Rulers of France
3. Julius Caesar

Current biography has been published since 1940 in monthly paperback form (except August), and in bound yearbook form which combines and replaces the contents of the monthly publications for one year.

This publication gives biographical summaries of people in the news. Long articles are written in an interesting style, and photographs of the celebrated personages are presented. People in all fields—science, politics, agriculture, motion pictures, music—are included. The coverage is national and international.

Current Biography also has a cumulative index. The index cumulates in each of the monthly issues for one year. In turn, the index in each yearbook cumulates for a ten-year period. The date of the yearbook and the dates included by the cumulative index in any particular volume are always labeled clearly on the outside of that volume.

Who's Who in America is published biennially and serves as a directory of important living Americans. Occasionally, a few prominent foreign names are included. The information given under each name is brief. Many abbreviations are used; these are explained in the front of the book.

Who Was Who in America contains biographies only for people who were in *Who's Who in America* before they died. Volume 1 contains biographies of people who died between 1897 and 1942, and volume 2 contains biographies for those who died between 1943 and 1950.

Practice 131

In which reference book would you look up the following people?

1. John Wayne
2. John Quincy Adams
3. John Fitzgerald Kennedy
4. John D. Rockefeller, Jr.
5. John Paul Jones

Atlases. An atlas is a collection of maps. Some of the most frequently used atlases are:

> *Encyclopaedia Britannica World Atlas*
> *Goode's World Atlas*
> *Hammond's Ambassador World Atlas*
> *Rand McNally Cosmopolitan World Atlas*
> Adams, James: *Atlas of American History*

Hammond, C. S.: *March of Civilization in Maps and Pictures*
Lord, Clifford: *Historical Atlas of the United States*

There are many types of atlases: world atlases, atlases for a
particular country or state, historical atlases, and others. There
are also many different kinds of maps in atlases:

physical, showing the highlands and lowlands in color
political, showing the boundaries of countries by a color
scheme
economic, showing how people make their living in different
localities

There are also climatic maps, population maps, vegetation maps,
and communications maps. Each map usually has a key, or
legend, in the corner of the page explaining the symbols and
colors.

In the back of each atlas, there is an index where you can find
the page (or plate) number of the map for which you are looking. In addition, there are marginal letters and figures indicating
the location on the page of the particular city, lake, or river for
which you are looking. Often, population figures are stated in the
index.

In some atlases, you will find latitudinal and longitudinal indications in the index instead of the letter and figure. The index is
a pronouncing index.

Most atlases include charts and tables on many subjects: world
comparisons, statistics on national resources, and production. A
list of abbreviations can be found usually just in front of the
index in each atlas.

On most maps, all political names are written in roman type.
Physical features are set in italic type. National capitals and state
capitals are written in large, heavy type and usually have a star
or star within a circle beside the name of the city.

Reader's Guide to Periodical Literature.   This reference gives
an index to magazine articles. The *Reader's Guide* enables you to
find easily the information you want in the back issues of magazines that the library has on file. Many magazines are useful to

students who are engaged in reference work, especially since a magazine often contains current information not yet published in book form.

The *Abridged Reader's Guide* is published once a month in paperback form. Every few months some of the issues are combined. Once a year a bound volume comes out, replacing the paper issues for the year. Every two years a larger volume is published combining two annual volumes.

The magazine articles are indexed by the author, if known, and by the subject. Dramas, operas, and stories are listed by title as well, with a *see* reference to the names of the authors and composers, where complete information is given. Motion pictures are indexed only under the heading *Moving picture plays*. The authors, subjects, and titles are arranged alphabetically, and each page is divided into two columns. The authors, subjects, and first words of titles are written in heavy, black type.

Many abbreviations are used in the *Reader's Guide*. A list of all the magazines indexed and their abbreviations is in the front of each copy. Right next to this list is the key to all the other abbreviations used.

THE BOOK REPORT

For many of the books that you read in the library, you may be asked to write a book review. In this section you will learn some of the ways to present such reviews, both written and oral.

In many ways, the written report differs little from the oral report. You will want to give much of the same information, the title of the book, the author, the subject matter, and the particular interest it has for you and for other potential readers. When you read a book, it is well to jot down a few notes to remind you of these details, since it may be difficult to obtain the book later on if you need that information.

Your teacher will undoubtedly indicate to you the form in which she wishes you to prepare your paper. Reports may vary from book to book in length, coverage, and perhaps even in the basic approach you use. For some books, you may be asked to give a general summary of what you read; whereas for others you may have some specific point that you are to bring out, such as the plot, the setting, the characterization, or perhaps some special knowledge that reading the book has given you. Whatever form you use or approach you take, there are several things to remember about book reviewing in general.

First of all, writing about a book requires the same kind of careful planning that writing for any purpose requires. If you think out in advance what it is you want to say, your paper will show it. Often, the notes that you jot down as you read will help you immensely in this way.

A paper on any aspect of a book should not attempt to be complete. If you choose to tell about the characters, pick one or two of the most interesting and discuss them in a way which will interest your readers, but which will not tell so much that their attention wanders. If you are telling about the plot of the book, do not attempt to outline the entire sequence of events. Usually, one or two of the most important, interesting, or exciting events will catch the attention of your reader and make him want to read the book for himself. Any summary of the plot should describe the basic situation and, perhaps, something of the complications, but almost never should you give away the ending.

Finally, your own reaction to a book is perhaps the most important part of your paper. In many ways, it is also the most difficult to write. Many times we read a book that satisfies us tremendously, but we are not always sure quite why it does. A little thought, however, will usually turn up some reasons for our judgment. Is the book well written, that is, does the author manage to hold our interest throughout without losing us in excessive detail, description, or side matters? If the book is a novel, is the plot a reasonable one? Do you feel that it could have happened? If it is a science-fiction book or a fantasy, does the improbability bother you? Are the characters interesting and lifelike? Is the book thoughtful? Is it about something important? Does it *matter*?

Remember, too, that your paper does not have to present a

favorable impression on your part. You are only required to make your summary factual and thoughtful, but you should be honest in your evaluation of the book. If you decide you do not like it, your reasons should be as convincing as those you give if you do like the book.

The oral book report. Many times you will speak book reports rather than write them. In these cases, you should prepare just as thoroughly as you would for a written report. There are, first of all, a number of important facts about the book you should mention. You should tell the title, the author, the subject matter, whether it is fiction or nonfiction, something about its level of difficulty, and whether its appeal is for boys or girls.

Do not relate the entire plot. Give enough in the way of interesting, exciting, or amusing incidents to whet the appetite of your hearers. Telling too much defeats one of your purposes, that of arousing enough interest in the book to make your listeners want to read it themselves.

Sometimes, although not always, some facts about the author can be valuable. Here again, do not give every detail you know, but rather those items which make the book itself more attractive. You may wish to give titles of other books he has written.

Finally, give some sort of personal evaluation of the book. "It was good" or "I liked it" will help, but not very much. Were the characters interesting, was there too much or too little description, and were you satisfied with the outcome of the story? If the book was nonfiction, did it present facts of biography, or history, or science in an interesting and informative way? Did it seem authentic and dependable?

Oral book reports are usually fairly short. Most would take only about five to ten minutes. Seldom if ever would anyone continue for as long as twenty minutes or half an hour.

Telling a story. Sometimes you will have oral composition work in which you tell a story. It may be an original story or it may be telling in your own words another's story. Here are some pointers about doing this type of oral work.

Whenever possible, your opening statement should capture the imagination of your listeners. Some people use an anecdote or a humorous part of the story to start. Remember, if you use this device, don't spoil it by laughing or getting the giggles when you tell it; play it straight.

Study the details you are going to present. Remember, story-telling does not have to be fictional, for many stories that are factual are just as interesting—perhaps more so—as those that are strictly fiction. In any case, select one of the most interesting facts or incidents for your opener. For example, if you were making a report on, or telling a story concerned with, dates—the kind that grow on trees—you might begin by asking, "What do you know about the private life of a date?" If you listen and watch carefully the next time you look at a television drama, you will notice the way the opening scene makes generous use of exciting material to capture your attention. You can use the same idea to capture the attention of your audience. But don't be *too* eager, and don't resort to cheap tricks. You can get an audience's attention by making funny faces, but this is no way to begin any kind of serious oral presentation.

If it is an experience, your own or someone else's, that you are relating, be sure to give the most important details right away. These details can be thought of as the *who, what, when,* and *where* of the incident or experience. *Who* is involved, *what* happened, *when* did it happen, and *where* did it happen? These are all questions your audience needs answered before you become involved in your presentation.

Thus, who are the characters? Are they young, are they unusual in any way, and are they people of whom your audience has heard? Make them come alive for your audience.

Set the time and place of your story. If the time is now, you don't need to say much. But if the incident occurred years ago or is set in the future, you will need to supply some details for the audience. What time of day was it? Was it winter or summer? Then, where did the experience take place? Picture the important details as much as necessary. Was it in the mountains, at the seashore, in a desert, a swamp, a city? Was it raining, sunny, warm, cold?

What happened? Give a sketch of the important events, with those details that are essential. Be careful not to overuse the pronoun "I." Your audience is interested in a story about people, not just you, even if you are the principal character in the story.

Finally, leave your audience interested by using a strong ending. Sometimes it is far more difficult to end a talk than it is to begin. Indeed, many speakers (both young and old) frequently make two serious errors. One is talking too long, and the other is ending too abruptly. Planning ahead can help avoid both pitfalls. Your presentation should be long enough to cover the topic well. It should not exhaust the audience by being too long, or confuse them by stopping short.

Practice 132

Prepare a short talk for your class. Tell them of an experience you had that was frightening, unpleasant, humorous, or amusing. When you give the talk, observe the people in the audience. Are they interested? Are they sharing your emotions? Are you successful in your effort to communicate with them? Are they "receiving" the message you are "sending"? What suggestions have they for improvement of your presentation?

If possible, or practical, use pictures or demonstration models to add interest to your talk. Having something to show may also give you more poise as you speak.

Index